MW00723591

Legal Issues
for Texas Teachers

Mark Littleton, Ed.D.
Tarleton State University

KENDALL/HUNT PUBLISHING COMPANY
4050 Westmark Drive   Dubuque, Iowa 52002

Dedication

I have the good fortune of being part of two wonderful families. This book is dedicated to both. The family who raised me and guided me in the direction of right and wrong, and taught me the difference between good and bad left their positive indelible impressions upon me. To my mother, father, and sisters, I will be eternally grateful.

The family that I helped raise with my wife, Pam, will forever be in my heart. I hope that I've left similar positive impressions upon my daughters--Rebecca, Stephanie, and Tiffany.

Contents

Preface

Seminars and workshops that I delivered to student teachers provided the inspiration for this book. Further inspired by students in my graduate school law course who often commented "all teachers need this stuff" I affirmed my commitment to assist teachers, particularly beginning teachers, with relevant legal issues. As I prepared for the book and during its creation, I often struggled with the topics and the amount of content to be included.

Teacher preparation programs are consumed with topics on instructional methodology, classroom management, curriculum planning, and a myriad of other topics important to teaching. It seems that there is little space in the preparation program to discuss legal issues. I did not want to add to an already crowded teacher preparation curriculum, but I did not want to miss addressing topics important to teachers already in the classroom. What is printed in this text is the result of that struggle.

This book is designed for student teachers, teacher interns, beginning teachers, and experienced teachers new to Texas classrooms. However, teachers with years of teaching in the Texas public school classrooms will also find it useful. Esoteric legal topics are avoided unless they are important to the content of the book. Legal terminology is also avoided. However, the book is academic in nature. Included are numerous references to statutes, legal treatises, and educational articles apropos to the content of the book. For those interested in further study, these references should prove to be quite useful.

A second edition of this book will follow only if it is useful to the reader. I encourage readers to submit suggestions to me (via the email below or through Kendall/Hunt) on the book's usefulness and to provide suggestions on topics that should be included or deleted.

Mark Littleton
Mlittleton@tarleton.edu
May 1, 2001

Acknowledgments

Many good people helped me with this book, and I would be terribly remiss not to acknowledge their assistance. Graduate assistants Amanda Truss, Lisa Nelson, and Louise Nelson provided valuable assistance at every turn. Also, Kim Pack deserves a gracious "thank you" for her review and frank comments.

Finally, I must thank my wife, Pam, who reviewed, edited, and endured several versions of each chapter.

Legal Issues for Texas Teachers

Introduction

On a daily basis, teachers are faced with issues that have the potential of leading them to the courts (Petzko, 2001). Whether we like it or not, "the role of law in education is increasing" (Redfield, 2000, p. 5). Certainly, no one expects teachers to have formal legal training; however, an understanding of relevant topics is very useful to the classroom teacher. This book does not attempt to cover all aspects of school law. It does, however, focus on those areas of school law that are most relevant to the classroom teacher.

Before a discussion of legal issues can take place, it is important to understand where law comes from. The first source of law is constitutional law. The constitution is a document that broadly outlines the philosophical basis for government. The U.S. Constitution, through its amendments, ensures that each individual in our society is granted certain freedoms (e.g., speech, religion), and provides protection from unfair treatment. However, the U.S. Constitution makes no provision for public education; therefore it is the responsibility of each state to provide an education for the public. The Texas Constitution places the duty of providing for an "efficient" system of education on the shoulders of the state legislature.

The state legislature provides the second source of law – statutory law. Through the Texas Education Code (TEC), the legislature delegates responsibilities to various institutions (e.g., the Texas Education Agency, the State Board of Education) and individuals (Commissioner of Public Education, superintendent, etc.) to conduct the business of educating students for the state. In Texas, the legislature meets every two years, therefore these laws, or statutes, are subject to modification on a biennial basis.

Some of the individuals or institutions charged (by the legislature) to carry out the business of public education have the authority to establish rules and regulations. These rules and regulations make up the third source of law–administrative law. Administrative law is not actual law (statutory), but carries the force and effect of actual law. In this book, references to administrative law will be either the Texas Administrative Code (TAC) or local school board policy.

Because of its high profile nature, case law, the fourth source of law, is probably the most familiar. After years of watching television shows like Perry Mason, Ben Matlock, and Judge Judy, the public is well aware of how the courts affect the legal system. In the courts, individuals may be prosecuted for breaking an enacted statute in the criminal courts, or be sued by another party in the civil courts.

While reading this book, it will be helpful to keep in mind the following six rules. Upon occasion, a reference to one of the rules will be made to help clarify a concept. As will be obvious, the rules are not "hard and fast." In fact, the point of the rules is to show that law is often ambiguous.

Rule Number 1 - Not all law is good law. Laws are "rules of action or conduct prescribed by controlling authority…which must be obeyed and followed by citizens subject to sanctions or legal consequences" (*Black's Dictionary of Law*, 1979, p. 795). Typically, laws are enacted to establish guidelines or to clarify previously written statutes (See Alexander & Alexander, 2001, pp. 4-5). However, the practical application is not always "good" in all situations. Fortunately, policymakers generally rewrite laws that do not provide the desired effect. As you read through this book, you may encounter some aspect of law that you deem "bad" law. From a legal perspective, the job of a classroom teacher is not to make the determination that the law is bad and therefore should not be followed. The teacher is obliged to comply with the law. Changing the law is another topic entirely, and it is not within the scope of this book.

Rule Number 2 - Just because something is legal, it does not mean that it is "right." The Texas Education Code is written to provide guidance for school officials, and it fails to cover every aspect of the daily operation of public schools. With a few exceptions, it does not indicate what teacher behavior is acceptable or unacceptable. As a result, educators in Texas have an Educator's Code of Ethics, which attempts to provide guidance to the behavior that is "right." Chapter 6 discusses the code of ethics and if the reader feels that some part of the law is not "right," appropriate educator actions are likely outlined in the code of ethics.

Rule Number 3 - A teacher can be disciplined for doing what is legal. This rule is the sibling to Rule Number 2. As you read through this book, you are cautioned not to believe that an act is acceptable if law does not prohibit it. The TEC does not direct the teacher to be in the classroom during every minute of instructional time. However, a teacher who leaves class during instructional time to attend to personal business may well be reprimanded or even fired! To keep out of trouble, the teacher should closely adhere to the next rule.

Rule Number 4 - Know the district's policies and follow them. The district's legal counsel or the Texas Association of School Boards typically scrutinizes district policies. District policies must comport with state and federal statutes. Additionally, local district policies are a form of administrative law and district employees must conform to policy.

Rule Number 5 - A person can be sued for anything. "Going to court" has become a favorite pastime for many Americans. Teachers, like all citizens, may be sued (or threatened with a suit) for just about anything. However, a teacher will likely prevail in court when she or he acts within the scope of the law.

Rule Number 6 – Prevention is the best legal defense. If a legal question arises, contact an attorney. Heubert (1997) points out that there is a need for closer collaboration between educators and lawyers. He further notes that improving the relationship between the educator and the lawyer will result in fewer instances of litigation.

This book will reveal that teachers have more legal "freedom" than is often portrayed by the media. Teachers have considerable authority to operate the classroom in the manner they see fit, as long as the authority is not abused. On the other hand, there is a lot of "folk law" in our public schools. Folk law is not real law, but it is perceived to be real law. For example, the author knows of no Texas statute prohibiting the operation of a motor vehicle without shoes, but many people believe that it is illegal to drive with bare feet.

This book provides a general understanding of legal issues that face Texas teachers. It is not a complete legal analysis of the law or legal issues, and it is not a substitute for legal counsel. Any teacher who believes that he or she is in need of legal counsel should contact a licensed attorney.

Chapter 1 addresses teacher-student issues that teachers face on a daily basis. Teachers are consistently confronted with legal dilemmas relating to student discipline, reporting suspected child abuse and neglect, and the legal issues of administering medication.

Field trips, student transportation and other school activities are impacted greatly by statutes and the courts. Teachers interested in learning about how to address religion in the classroom or the fair use of copyrighted material would be wise to closely study Chapter 2.

The third chapter addresses an evolving field of litigation. Student-to-student and teacher-to-student sexual harassment is a major concern for parents, teachers, administrators, and students.

Chapter 4 lightly touches on the most highly litigated area of public education–that of special education. Beginning teachers are often unaware of their responsibility to special education students and to the regulations controlling programs for students with disabilities.

In Chapter 5 the law concerning student records is discussed. Every teacher should have a basic understanding of who has access to a student's educational records.

Recently, a great deal of discussion and policy making has surrounded ethics for educators. The State Board for Educator Certification (SBEC) continues to review and refine the Code of Ethics for Texas Educators and a major SBEC responsibility is investigating ethics complaints. Chapter 6 addresses the code of ethics and disciplinary procedures associated with reported ethics violations.

Chapter 7 includes a brief discussion of the types of contracts offered to Texas teachers. It concludes by offering teachers an insight to the certificate renewal process.

Chapter 1

Student Interactions

Introduction

School is all about students. It is about teaching them and helping them grow into productive citizens. As the teacher progresses through the school day, he or she will interact with students in various settings and at many different levels. In this chapter, legal issues regarding student discipline, reporting suspected child abuse or neglect, distribution of medication, and providing medical attention will be discussed. The focus of this chapter is clearly on the student.

Student Supervision

Although the primary purpose of the public schools is to educate children, regimenting and controlling their lives and behavior has become a dominant mission of the schools (Nogeura, 1995). Supervising students in an effort to maintain their safety and security has become increasingly complex. Horrific events such as those in Littleton, Colorado and Santee, California have created a sense of urgency on the part of schools officials to provide greater protection for students. Teachers bear considerable responsibility in the supervision of students and in controlling student behavior; and although teacher authority often appears to be limited by ludicrous rules and stifling regulations, teachers possess considerable authority and control over students. It is, however, important for teachers to understand their legal rights and legal limitations.

Student Discipline

There is a reasonable expectation that teachers will supervise students while the students are on the school campus

(Alexander and Alexander, 2001). A well-managed classroom will reduce the number of discipline problems and lead to student learning (Shalaway, 1997). Failure to properly supervise students may lead to poor classroom management and/or student injury. In Texas, laws regarding student discipline can be found in Chapter 37 of the Texas Education Code (TEC). Districts are required to have a written code of conduct developed by the district-level planning committee (TEC § 37.001[a]). The code of conduct must indicate the circumstances in which a student may be removed from the classroom or campus, and outline those conditions under which a student may be suspended (TEC, § 37.001 [a] [1-3]).

Classroom Management

Minor infractions. The vast majority of discipline problems that a teacher will confront are considered minor infractions of classroom rules and procedures. Although the law does not prescribe the manner in which a teacher must address the minor infractions, most teacher preparation programs have an extensive unit or entire course on classroom management activities. Kemerer and Walsh (2000) note that the manner in which minor infractions are addressed is "largely left to the local school district, administrators, and teachers" (p. 273).

Over time, teachers have developed a repertoire of intervention strategies to address minor infractions. The strategies include verbal reprimands, detentions, and parent conferences. Classroom management techniques vary widely, but generally require that the teacher 1) establish a few reasonable rules, 2) explain the need for the rules, 3) teach the rules, and 4) establish reasonable and logical consequences for breaking the rules (Emmer, et al., 1994; Charles, 1992; Wong and Wong, 1991). Kemerer and Walsh (2000) recommend that the rules have a rational and clear purpose, and prior to implementing the disciplinary action, the teacher should explain the infraction to the student and provide the student with an opportunity to explain his or her actions.

What would be an example of an inappropriate consequence for a minor infraction?

The media has a field day when teachers fail to use good judgment when dispensing punishment for minor infractions. A good example occurred in a south Texas school district a few years ago. The teacher placed the student in a time-out area when the student became agitated. Unfortunately, the time-out area was a box.

If a student talks out-of-turn, placing tape over the mouth is considered an unwise and inappropriate punishment.

Student Removal. One means of dealing with persistent infractions of classroom rules is to send the misbehaving student to the principal. Texas law actually provides for this technique (TEC § 3737.002[a]), but wily veterans of the classroom know that overuse of this technique diminishes the teacher's ability to control behavior.

Student removal from the classroom is generally reserved for an infraction of the student code of conduct or other serious incidents of misbehavior. Texas law allows a teacher to remove a student from the classroom when the student "repeatedly interferes with the teacher's ability to communicate" (TEC, § 37.002[b][1]), or is "so unruly, disruptive, or abusive that it seriously interferes with the teacher's ability to communicate" (TEC, § 37.002[b][2]).

Texas law requires the teacher to remove a student from the classroom when the student engages in conduct that the state considers very serious. The behaviors that require the teacher to remove the student from the class are listed in Figure 1.1. Again, the law REQUIRES the teacher to remove the student from the classroom, and a wise teacher heeds this requirement. As an example, a teacher who fails to remove a student for a terroristic threat ("I'm going to kill you!") under the belief that the threat was a joke, is likely to regret her choice not to follow through with the law.

Figure 1.1

Conduct Requiring Removal from the Class
(Texas Education Code, § 37.006)

- Any activity that is punishable as a felony
- An assault
- A terroristic threat
- Selling, giving, or delivering marijuana
- Selling, giving, or delivering dangerous drugs
- Selling, giving, or delivering an alcoholic beverage
- Abusing glue or aerosol paint
- Public lewdness or indecent exposure

Corporal Punishment

Although research on the effectiveness of corporal punishment has been inconclusive (Bitensky, 1999; Hyman, 1998), Imbrogno (2000) notes that "corporal punishment in American homes and schools is a well-entrenched tradition" (p. 127). Numerous organizations, such as the American Academy of Pediatrics, the American Counseling Association and the National Congress of Parents and Teachers, have called for the elimination of corporal punishment in our schools (Richardson and Wilcox, 1994). Corporal punishment has been linked to increased antisocial behavior (American Academy of Pediatrics, 2000; Kirchner, 1998), obsessive-compulsive behavior, depression, disassociation, and paranoia (Bitensky, 1999). Additionally, it has been linked to continuing practices of discrimination, where minority children receive a disproportionate amount of corporal punishment (Hyman, 1996; Nogeura, 1995; McFadden and Marsh, 1992; Slate and Perez, 1991). Once considered a perfectly acceptable form of discipline in our schools under the doctrine of *in loco parentis*–in the place of parents–(Weiss, 1996), corporal punishment is losing its appeal as a form of behavior management. What was once a

4

socially acceptable means of controlling student behavior is now often viewed as socially unacceptable (Edwards, 1996). Adams (2000) notes that "while this [corporal punishment] may have been successful with the one-room schoolhouse, it lost its effectiveness with large hierarchically structured schools" (142).

Vockell (1991) defines corporal punishment as "the infliction of physical pain contingent upon the occurrence of a misbehavior" (p. 278). In the context of the school, it is often interpreted to be the striking of the buttocks with a paddle. It may however, include pinching, running a required distance, or holding heavy objects. Even though the U.S. Supreme Court has determined that corporal punishment is not unconstitutional (*Ingraham v. Wright*, 1977), and that schools can utilize it as a means of punishment even if the parents object (*Baker v. Owen*, 1975), most states prohibit the use of corporal punishment (Essex, 1999). In a state like Texas where corporal punishment is not prohibited by the statutes, school boards closely regulate its use (Valente and Valente, 2001). Kemerer and Walsh (2000) note that "to lessen the chances of damage suits in state or federal courts, most schools specify that corporal punishment can be used only under certain circumstances and in accord with certain procedures" (p. 275).

Teachers, and other educators, who choose to utilize corporal punishment as a behavior management technique open themselves to criminal and civil charges (Stebler, Walsh, and Kemerer, 2000). Corporal punishment is one of the few areas where the teacher is not immune from civil prosecution. The Texas Education Code (TEC) § 22.051 states that a teacher

> Is not personally liable for any act…within the scope of the duties…that involves the exercises of judgment or discretion on the part of the employee [teacher], except in circumstances in which a professional employee uses excessive force in the discipline of students or negligence resulting in bodily injury to students.

It is generally agreed that teachers should avoid using corporal punishment as a means of behavior management. In the event that the teacher opts to use corporal punishment, the teacher should be specific in stating the behavior that may lead to corporal punishment and use it only as a last resort. It should be administered in front of a witness (another professional educator, preferably a school administrator), but out of the sight of other students. Parents must be notified of the punishment indicating the name of the witness and the reason for the punishment (Kemerer and Walsh, 2000). Most importantly, read the district policy manual and follow it (Rule Number 4).

As I read TEC 22.051 as written above, it appears that as a teacher, I cannot be held liable for injury to students if a fight occurs in my classroom. Can that be right?

The law does provide sweeping protection for teachers. It is quite possible, however, that a teacher who does not act within the scope of his or her duties may be held liable for injury to a student. As stated though, that protection does not extend to student discipline (corporal punishment). Don't forget that a teacher can be legal and still be disciplined for inappropriate actions (Rules Number 3).

Required Reports for Teachers

Texas law requires the building principal to submit reports to law enforcement authorities when a student violates certain provisions of the Penal and Health and Safety codes (TEC § 37.015). Furthermore, the teacher is required to submit a written report to the principal when a student violates the student code of conduct. The law (TEC § 37.001[b]) states

> A teacher with knowledge that a student has violated the student code of conduct shall file with the school principal or other appropriate administrator a written report, not to exceed one page, documenting the violation. The principal or other appropriate administrator shall, not later than 24 hours after receipt of a report from a teacher, send a copy of the report to the student's parents or guardians.

Many schools have devised standardized forms for the purpose of meeting this law. A copy of the form is then sent with the student (or by the postal system) to the parents. Teachers should know the school's procedure for completing this required report.

Reporting Child Abuse and Neglect

Although it is not as prevalent as it once was, child abuse is an alarming problem (Vital Statistics, 2001). In 1994, the Texas child protective services agency investigated over 109,000 reports of child abuse, and substantiated over 55,000 cases of abuse and neglect (Child Abuse and Neglect Fact Sheet, 2001). The actual instances of child abuse are probably much greater than reported incidents (Romeo, 2000; Sechrist, 2000). In fact, it is very likely that emotional abuse and neglect are underreported. Romeo (2000) reports that physical and sexual incidents are reported more frequently than emotional abuse, probably because the symptoms of emotional abuse are more difficult to identify. Perpetrators of this emotional abuse are usually the natural parents of the child (Sheppard, 1994).

Among other things, child abuse or neglect includes:

- Mental or emotional injury
- Physical injury
- Threat of physical harm
- Failure to reasonably prevent from harm
- Sexual conduct that is harmful to the child's emotional or physical welfare
- Failure to reasonably prevent sexual conduct harmful to the child
- Child obscenity
- Use or causing a child to use a controlled substance
- Leaving a child in a situation that would expose the child to harm

- Failure to seek or obtain medical care for a child in need of medical care, or
- Failure to provide a child with food, clothes, or shelter necessary to sustain life or health (*A Parent's Guide*, 2001).

Child abuse is not a federal crime (Fischer, Schimmel, and Kelly, 1999), but all states, explicitly or implicitly, have statutes prohibiting child abuse and neglect (Foreman and Bernet, 2000; Levesque, 2000). Foreman and Bernet (2000) note that these laws are often vague, and officials do not fully understand when they must report suspected abuse. In Texas, the law is clear. The Texas Family Code (TFC), Section 261.101 (b) states that:

> If a professional has cause to believe that a child has been abused or neglected or may be abused or neglected...the professional shall make a report not later than the 48th hour after the hour the professional first suspects that the child has been or may be abused or neglected.[1]

As noted earlier, determining whether or not child abuse exists is difficult (McGlinchey, Keenan, and Dillenburger, 2000). It is unfortunate that school officials typically exclude the identification of child abuse and neglect from training and professional development programs[2] (Hodgkinson and Baginsky, 2000; Sechrist, 2000). However, it is not the responsibility of the teacher to make a determination of the existence of child abuse or neglect. The teacher is required, by law, to report suspicion of child abuse or neglect within 48 hours to any local or state law enforcement agency, or the Department of Protective and

---

[1] Texas Family Code § 262.101 (b) specifically defines teachers as professionals.

[2] Legal definitions of child abuse and neglect are found at the website for the Texas Department of Protective and Regulatory Services (http://www.tdprs.state.tx.us). Romeo (2000) elaborates on symptoms of emotional abuse in the article *The educator's role in Reporting the Emotional Abuse of Children* in the September, 2000 issue of **The Journal of Instructional Psychology.**

Regulatory Services via the Texas Child Abuse Hotline (TFC § 261.103).

When a report is made, the teacher must provide 1) the name and address of the child, 2) the name and address of the person responsible for the child, and 3) any other information regarding the suspected abuse or neglect (TFC § 261.104). Reports are confidential[3] (TFC § 261.101 [d]), and teachers making the report in good faith are immune from civil or criminal liability (TFC § 261.106[a]). However, failure to report the suspected abuse or neglect is a misdemeanor (TFC § 261.109 [b]), and a teacher "may not delegate to or rely on another person to make the report" (TFC 261.101 [b]).

For more information on child protection, visit the website of the Texas Department of Protective and Regulatory Services at http://www.tdprs.state.tx.us. The Texas Child Abuse Hotline is open 24 hours each day, 7 days a week. The Hotline telephone number is 1-800-252-5400.

My school requires teachers to report suspected child abuse to the principal. Isn't this against the law?

Whether the policy is illegal is open to debate. It may be argued that such a practice is in violation of the law that protects the confidentiality of the person making the report. Teachers can, however, voluntarily report the suspected abuse or neglect to the principal. Texas law directs teachers to report suspected child abuse or neglect to law enforcement officials or to the child protective services agency via the telephone hotline. Additionally, the law indicates that teachers cannot delegate or rely on another to make the report.

---

[3] The reporting teacher can, and should, remain anonymous so that others are unable to identify the person making the report.

Medication and Medical Attention

The administration of medication to students is fraught with danger (Sesno, 1998). And, because of the ever-present danger of illegal drugs, schools are closely monitoring the distribution of medication. Once again, since each district's policies and procedures for the administration of medication are different, teachers would be especially wise to know the district's policies and follow them (Rule Number 4).

Texas law protects teachers from civil liability for damages resulting in the administration of medication as long as the injuries do not result from gross negligence[4]. The teacher should 1) have written permission from the parent, and 2) ensure that the prescription medication is in the original container with proper labeling (TEC § 22.052).

It is incumbent upon teachers to administer first-aid to students in need; but obviously, the school nurse provides better medical attention. On those occasions when the nurse is not present or immediate attention is needed, the teacher must act on the behalf of the student. Once first-aid is administered, the proper medical authorities should be contacted. Once again, training in basic first-aid is of utmost importance and should not be viewed as trivial.

Summary

Constant every-day interactions with students can leave a teacher exhausted. The teacher is responsible for supervision of students, maintaining effective discipline, reporting suspected abuse and neglect, and administering medication if appropriate. Teachers are not expected to be legal experts. However, prudent teachers will maintain a basic understanding of legal issues that face them daily. Teachers must be diligent and supervise students in the classroom, in the halls, in the cafeteria, and on the grounds. Often student misbehavior is controlled with quick, direct guidance. However, teachers must be willing to utilize more

---

[4] Gross negligence is an overt act or omission of a legal duty. It is more than the failure to exercise ordinary care (*Black's Dictionary of Law*, 1979).

stringent actions, (e.g., removal from the classroom) for more serious rule infractions.

During the supervisory activities, teachers must be cognizant of the signs of abuse and neglect. Once suspicion of abuse or neglect is aroused, then teachers must become advocates for the students and report their suspicions to the proper authorities. Far too often, abuse goes unreported.

Extended Thinking Activities

There was a lot of action at the high school yesterday. Two students got into a fight in Mr. Thomas's room and one was seriously injured. Apparently, Able grabbed a wooden ruler from the teacher's desk and stabbed another student, Payne, in the eye. Mr. Thomas was not in the room when the fight occurred. Fellow teachers in the east wing of the building have noticed Mr. Thomas, the science teacher, is often careless. He frequently leaves his class during instructional time. The students often joke that he goes to the boy's restroom to smoke a cigarette or to the teacher's workroom to eat a snack. Student rumors do not appear to be true, but yesterday Mr. Thomas was seen visiting with the school counselor while class was in session. Angel, Payne's girlfriend, is telling her friends that Payne's parents are going to sue Mr. Thomas, the counselor, the principal, and the school district for negligence.

1. Can Payne's parents sue Mr. Thomas, the counselor, the principal and the school? What are their chances of success? What are the possible repercussions for Mr. Thomas?

2. If a fellow teacher told you that he or she suspected that a particular student was being physically abused, what would be your obligation to the teacher? Even if you had no reason to suspect abuse prior to visiting with the other teacher, would you be obligated to report the suspected abuse?

Chapter 2

School Activities

Introduction

School is clearly about the interaction between the teacher and the student. As discussed in Chapter 1, the interaction occurs in many different venues. This chapter will continue the discussion of the teacher-student interaction, but the focus will be on the school activity. Specifically, this chapter discusses legal issues that pertain to field trips, student transportation, and copyright laws.

Field Trips

Classroom instruction is often greatly enhanced by taking students on field trips. Yet, field trips are fraught with risks. Teachers who use field trips to supplement classroom instruction are often concerned about liability issues that may accompany such ventures. Except for student transportation issues that will be discussed later, liability for teachers on field trips is much the same as that in the classroom.

Schools usually require students to have parents complete an off-campus activity form prior to the trip. The forms generally require the parents to give their permission for the student to attend a specific off-campus activity at a given location on a specific day. Additionally, the document often asks for information regarding special medical needs and provides for parental permission to seek necessary medical attention in case of medical necessity. Although these forms do not release the teacher from any responsibility related to the supervision of students, it does 1) inform the parents of the date, time and location of the trip, and 2) provide consent for emergency medical treatment.

Student Transportation

School districts transport students for two purposes. First, districts transport students to and from school on established bus routes. These routes are established by the school district and the Texas Education Agency and districts are reimbursed for the costs of transporting eligible students. Contrary to popular opinion, school districts are not required to transport students to and from school (Texas Education Code [TEC], 34.007[a]). However, most districts choose to do so.

Second, school districts transport students to extra-curricular activities, field trips, and other school-related activities. This is often an expensive activity that requires considerable district-wide coordination and support. Often school districts develop procedures for securing school buses for transporting students.

Transporting students is one of the few areas where teachers open themselves to civil liability. Texas law provides that civil immunity for educators does not extend "to the operation, use, or maintenance of any motor vehicle" (TEC, § 22.051 [b]). As a result, teachers who use school or personal vehicles should be aware that injuries resulting from transporting students may lead to lawsuits involving considerable damage awards against the teacher and the district.

District policies regarding student transportation are often very specific. When a teacher transports 15 or more students to any school activity (other than bus routes), only school buses (or other motor buses) may be used. Passenger cars or vans may be used if fewer than 15 students are going to be transported (TEC, § 34.003 [b]). Furthermore, no student may stand while a bus or van is in motion (TEC, § 34.004).

I coach basketball and I often have students who do not have a ride home after a game. Should I take the student home?

You probably should increase your personal liability coverage if you routinely transport students in your own vehicle. In any event, avoid transporting students in those instances. Not only could you be faced with liability issues related to transportation, but there are also UIL rules that you may be violating. To assist the student, work with the student's relatives or local law enforcement officers when necessary.

Persons who drive school buses must possess a commercial driver license (CDL), and undergo 20 hours of school bus driver training. The bus driver must pass a written examination, an air brake test, and a driving test. Additionally, the Department of Transportation requires the drug testing of school bus drivers (Kemerer and Walsh, 2000). Other than possessing a valid Texas driver's license, the state does not mandate minimum standards for transporting students in passenger vehicles or vans. However, school districts often have additional requirements for operation of these vehicles, and teachers who wish to transport students would be wise to locate (and follow) district policies (Rule Number 4).

Copyright

Copyright laws affect teachers each school day. The idea that teachers are exempt from copyright laws when presenting information in the classroom is folk law. Although it is uncommon for teachers to intentionally violate copyright laws, teachers must understand that they are not exempt from the copyright laws (Brown, 1996; Thomas, 1992). Teachers do have the right to a "fair use" of copyrighted material (20 U.S.C. § 107), but the courts continue to have difficulty deciding what fair use is (Griffith, 1998). There are, however, some guidelines for teachers to follow.

Videotaping

Occasionally, a teacher will choose to enhance a particular lesson by replaying a tape-recorded commercial television program. Such practice appears to fall under the fair use doctrine. Fischer, Schimmel, and Kelly (1999) note that teachers "may keep the tape for only forty-five days," and can use it for instructional purposes during the first 10 days. At the end of the 45 day period, the tape must be erased or destroyed (p. 140). However, programs that can be purchased or rented may fall outside of the fair use doctrine. It is important to note that "when an instructor rents or purchases a tape, he or she should not duplicate the tape" (Brown, 1996, p. 88).

Figure 2.1

Copyright Wrongs

- Videos labeled FOR HOME VIEWING ONLY should not be shown at school
- Computer software purchased for school purposes should not be used on the home computer
- Consumable materials, such as workbooks, should not be copied
- Anthologies should not be developed without obtaining permission for each of the collected works

---

Printed Material

Teachers may make a single copy of a part of a book, newspaper article, or magazine article for the purpose of preparing for a class (Fischer, Schimmel, and Kelly, 1999). A congressional committee established guidelines for the multiple reproduction of materials for classroom use (Imber and van Geel, 2000; Gomez and Craycraft, 1998). Multiple copies may be used if they contain

- No more than 250 words of a poem,
- A complete article or essay that is less than 2,500 words,
- No more than 10% or 2 pages of an excerpt from any work, or
- A single chart or illustration from a book (Imber and van Geel, 2000; Kemerer and Walsh, 2000; Fowler, Henslee, and Hepworth, 1998; Gomez and Craycraft, 1998; Thomas, 1992).

Additionally, use of multiple copies must be for only one course in the school, and there should be no more than nine instances of multiple copying during any semester of a course (Gomez and Craycraft, 1998). Teachers should avoid creating "anthologies," the publishing of a collection of created works. Teachers are cautioned not make multiple copies of consumable materials.

Our school is experiencing a budget cut. Is it legal to purchase a classroom set of workbooks and reproduce them for other classes?

In a word, the answer is NO. Material that is considered "public domain" may be copied without risk. However, workbooks are consumable and very few are public domain.

Electronic Media

Piracy of computer software is strictly prohibited. When computer software is purchased, the buyer simply purchases a license to use the software. Schools may purchase a site license for the software, which allows the use of the software on multiple machines. However, unless the license agreement specifically states otherwise, schools are not authorized to purchase a single copy of the software to distribute among the staff (Fowler, Henslee, and Hepworth, 1998).

With the advent of the Internet, copyright laws are being revisited. It appears that information downloaded from the Internet is subject to copyright laws and the fair use doctrine just as hard copy materials are. Copyrighted information downloaded from the Internet and kept electronically should be deleted (or erased) after use, and should not be used "outside the classroom for non-educational uses" (Aldridge, 1998, p. 3).

Religion and Prayer

The First Amendment to the U.S. Constitution states that "Congress shall make no law respecting an establishment of religion, or prohibiting the free exercise thereof." These seemingly conflicting clauses have led to emotional debates and landmark court cases addressing the interaction between government and religion. On one hand, through the Establishment Clause government is expressly prohibited from supporting religion. On the other hand, through the Free Exercise clause, government is expressly prohibited from keeping individuals from engaging in religious practices. As a consequence, the government is directed to maintain neutrality in its interaction with religious organizations and religious practices (*Lemon v. Kurtzman*, 1971).

Public schools are an arm of the state. Alexander and Alexander (2001) note that "public schools of America are secular and not merely nonsectarian; this is necessary if separation of church and state is to be complete" (p. 145). Schools must not proscribe or support any particular religion or religious practice and cannot "encroach on religious beliefs of the individual," but still they are not to appear "godless" (p. 145). Consequently, schools must be cautious when dealing with religious issues.

Prayer

Texas law (TEC, § 25.082) allows school districts to begin each class day with a time for the student to "reflect or meditate." However, a prudent teacher will check with the school principal to determine school policy or procedure prior to allowing time for this activity. Teachers should avoid leading students in Bible reading, prayer, or other devotional activities (See *Engel v. Vitale*, 1962; and *Abington v. Schempp*, 1963). Murray and Evans (2000) recommend that school personnel not "indicate actively or passively a time for prayer or 'private meditation" (p. 81). However, a student who chooses to silently pray or meditate without disrupting school activities should be allowed to do so (Brown and Gilbert, 1996).

The recent high-profile court case *Santa Fe ISD v. Doe* (2000) led to considerable emotional debate throughout Texas. In this case, the U.S. Supreme Court held that a school district's policy of school-sponsored prayer at high school football games, even if it is student-led, was a violation of the Establishment Clause. Kemerer and Walsh (2000) note that "the law is clear that neither the public school nor its employees may sponsor prayer at school or at extracurricular activities and athletic events" (p. 233).

Religion

Religion and religious discussions permeate every part of the curriculum taught in public schools. Music history is filled with classic pieces based upon religion. Much of the history of the U.S. and world has been shaped by the impact of religion. Classical literature is replete with religion and religious overtones.

Much of what I teach is based upon the actions of religious people. Am I suppose to avoid important curricular concepts to avoid litigation?

Schools and school officials are prohibited from supporting religious activities or endorsing a particular religion. Schools must remain neutral. However, there is no indication that teachers are to be hostile toward religion, and certainly teachers are not expected to avoid discussions regarding religion's impact on the curriculum. For example, it would be very difficult for a history teacher to discuss the Crusades and avoid any discussion about religion.

Teaching about religion is certainly different than promoting a religion. Gomez and Craycraft (1998) note that "[r]eligion can be discussed in class if it is part of the curriculum. The Bible may be taught as literature, and comparison of various religions may be made as long as the purposes are secular" (p. 150). Art and music are filled with religious themes and can be studied. Teachers must understand that they are very influential and as actors for the state, they must neither advance nor inhibit a particular religion or religious belief. As one parent stated, "I send my child to the church of choice because I want him to grow in that faith, but I can't make that choice with his teacher."

Summary

Transportation received attention in this chapter because of the liability associated with the operation of motor vehicles. Teachers who transport students must obtain all possible training and closely adhere to local board policy.

With the advent of the Internet, copyright laws are attracting more attention than in the recent past. Teachers are not exempt from copyright laws and often violate them unwittingly. Teachers can expect schools to be monitored more closely in the future particularly as copyright laws pertain to the Internet, computer software, and videos continue to be challenged.

Religion and prayer in the classroom receive considerable attention in the media. This is probably due to the interrelationship between religion and school that has evolved over the past 200 years. It is certainly an emotional issue and one fraught with enough political danger that each teacher should give it considerable thought prior to introducing religion or prayer into the activities of the classroom.

Extended Thinking Activities

The students have been working very hard to prepare for taking the TAAS test. Finally, the week of the tests has arrived. The tests were given on Tuesday, Wednesday, and Thursday, and the students took the tests seriously and performed admirably. As a reward for their hard work and diligent preparation, the teacher, Sara McGillicuty, promised them a "free day." On the free day, Ms. McGillicuty rented a video from the local video store to show to the class on Friday morning.

1. Do you think Ms. McGillicuty violated copyright laws?

2. Could there have been a "free day" activity that would be more appropriate to a school setting and less likely to run afoul of copyright laws?

Chapter 3

Sexual Harassment

Introduction

Don't tolerate sexual abuse: Stop It Now! Those words can be found on signs on college campuses all across the country. While the subject of this book is the public school setting, the sign is emblematic of society's increased awareness and concern about sexual harassment. "Sexual harassment is a serious and pervasive problem in society" (Note, 2000, p. 301). Behavior that once was tolerated by society is no longer socially acceptable, and it interferes with student academic performance (Harris and Grooms, 2000; Hutchison, 2000).

Legal issues regarding sexual harassment are still in the evolutionary stage, particularly in the public school setting. The Code of Federal Regulations defines sexual harassment as "conduct that has the purpose or effect of unreasonably interfering with an individual's work performance or creating an intimidating, hostile, or offensive work environment" (29 CFR § 1604.11). Obviously, this statute focuses on sexual harassment in the workplace. Considering the school setting, the U.S. Department of Education (USDOE) (2000) defines sexual harassment as

> unwelcome sexual advances, requests for sexual favors, and other verbal, nonverbal, or physical conduct of a sexual nature by an employee, by another student, or by a third party that is sufficiently severe, persistent, or pervasive to limit a student's ability to participate in or benefit from an education program or activity, or to create a hostile or abusive environment. (p. 1524)

The definition appears to be vague and cumbersome. Yet, combined with case law, there are enough specifics in the definition to provide assistance and guidance to teachers. It is important that teachers are knowledgeable of sexual harassment law (Note, 2000).

Types of Sexual Harassment

There are two federal statutes that address sexual harassment issues. The first, Title VII of the Civil Rights Act of 1964, is an employment statute, which prohibits discrimination on the basis of sex in the work place (Hairston, 1998). The second, Title IX of the Education Amendments of 1972, is an educational statute, which prohibits disparate treatment of individuals in educational institutions on the basis of sex (Grooms and Harris; 2000; Williams, 1999). Employee-to-employee sexual harassment is addressed by Title VII, where Title IX addresses employee-to-employee, employee-to-student, and student-to-student (Alexander and Alexander, 2000).

Sexual harassment can be categorized in several ways. This chapter will discuss sexual harassment issues from two different viewpoints. First, there will be a discussion of the types of legal causes of action. Second, there will be discussion from an institutional perspective.

Legal Causes of Action

Quid pro quo. The exchange of sexual favors for a desired benefit is called quid pro quo harassment (USDOE, 2000). Alexander and Alexander (2000) define quid pro quo harassment as that "by which the teacher, administrator, or other person in power attempts to compel submission to sexual demands by conditioning rewards or punishment upon the student's acquiescence or lack thereof" (p. 368). This type of sexual harassment implies a power relationship between the harasser and the victim. For example, in the school setting, it could be that a teacher (harasser) awards a grade on the provision that the student (victim) grants sexual favors. The power relationship may exist between the supervisor and a teacher as well (a positive evaluation from the supervisor in return for sexual favors).

What are sexual favors?

Good question. Sexual favors can include kissing, touching, or more invasive acts of a sexual nature.

Hostile environment. Hairston (1998) notes that those guilty of hostile environment harassment usually engage "in language, touching, and other forms of sexually-related conduct, which make the victim's ... life miserable" (p. 2). In *Davis v. Monroe County Board of Education* (1997), LaShonda Davis was the victim of constant sexual harassment from a classmate. The harasser constantly touched her inappropriately, and made sexually suggestive comments. As a result of the harassment, LaShonda's grades deteriorated, and she even contemplated suicide. Clearly, LaShonda was in a hostile environment.

For hostile environment sexual harassment to exist, the conduct must be pervasive or severe or objectively offensive (Williams, 1999). Single incidents of teasing and offensive jokes seldom rise to the level of severe, however one court ruled that a single slap on the buttocks was sufficiently pervasive to be considered harassment (Imber and van Geel, 2000).

Types of Institutional Sexual Harassment

Employee-to-employee. Typically, employee-to-employee sexual harassment complaints are addressed through the Title VII statute. Harris and Grooms (2000) remind us that "since Justice Thomas' confirmation hearing in 1991, much public debate and discussion has focused on sexual harassment issues" (p. 576).

In the employee-to-employee relationship, the behavior must be unwelcome for it to be considered harassment. Imber and van Geel (2000) further note that "the harassed person must not have solicited the behavior and must have communicated to the harasser that the behavior was not desired" (p. 340).

Employee-to-student. Employee-to-student sexual harassment is far too common in Texas public schools. A recent review of the docket of the Texas State Board for Educator Certification[1] revealed that approximately 10% of all certification-related disciplinary issues were related to employee-to-student sexual conduct issues. Touching that was once viewed as comforting and reassuring is now often viewed as touch with a sexual motive or innuendo.

Franklin v. Gwinnett County Public Schools (1992), *Doe v. Taylor* (1994), and *Gebser v. Lago Vista* (1998), established guidelines for employee-to-student sexual harassment. The courts have determined that a student sexually harassed by an employee can receive monetary damages.

Is it inappropriate to touch a student?

Not necessarily. However, with the increased awareness and concern over inappropriate sexual actions, teachers must be cognizant of what is appropriate and what is not. Shaking hands, and "high fives" are two means of non-sexual, non-aggressive touch. Generally, hugging an elementary child to comfort a deflated ego is appropriate. However, a male secondary teacher who places his arms around a female secondary student should be aware that such behavior is likely to be viewed as unacceptable in any community.

Student-to-student. Student-to-student harassment, or peer sexual harassment has been around for many years (Note, 2000). Actions that once were viewed as "innocent teasing" or actions previously attributed to "boys will be boys" may now be considered sexual harassment (Hutchison, 2000). Stein (1995) suggests that "the antecedents of peer sexual harassment in schools

---

[1] The State Board for Educator Certification (SBEC) investigates complaints about teachers (and other educators) who engage in inappropriate relationships with students. Teachers found guilty of engaging in an inappropriate relationship with a student may lose their certification.

may be found in 'bullying'—behavior children learn, practice, and experience at a very young age."

Sexual harassment is not necessarily male-to-female. Sexual harassment may be female-to-male, or same-sex harassment. Sexually explicit taunts, sexual graffiti, or rumors may be considered sexual harassment (Stein, 1995).

Avoiding Sexual Harassment Complaints

Harris and Groom (2000) note that while the courts have been "instructive, they do not explicitly clarify the day-to-day responsibilities, duties, and expectations of ... teachers" (p. 578). Teachers must, however, respond to complaints of sexual harassment (Note, 2000; Williams, 1999), and it is wise to do so in an expedient manner (Robinson, 1996). Each school is required to have a grievance procedure for students who make sexual harassment complaints (34 CFR 106.8[b]), and prevention programs should be developed with appropriate disciplinary actions for occurrences of sexual harassment (Note, 2000).

It is best to deal with sexual harassment issues before they get to the legal system (Stein, 1995). According to Hairston (1998), "the key to preventing sexual harassment ... is to have good policies and reporting procedures and to follow and enforce them" (p. 20). Williams (1999) notes that the policies should contain

- Training in the procedures for addressing harassment complaints
- Identification of sexually harassing behaviors
- Investigation procedures, and
- Appropriate disciplinary actions

Teachers may be held liable if they are aware of the sexual harassment, but fail to do anything about it. When a teacher observes a clearly obvious need for action, but provides "a woefully inadequate response," the courts could determine that the teacher is "deliberately indifferent" (Williams, 1999, p. 1103).

So, what can the teacher do to stop the harassment?

First, the teacher should use his or her authority to stop the immediate action. Second, implement disciplinary actions as indicated in the code of conduct to discourage future behaviors. Finally, monitor the behavior of the harasser to prevent future occurrences of sexual harassment.

Furthermore, it is important that teachers respond to sexually harassing situations in "all of the school's operations, including academic, educational, extra-curricular, and athletic programs" (Groom and Harris, 2000, p. 580).

Summary

Not only are sexual harassment claims common in schools, the numbers appear to be increasing. In an attempt to address valid claims, school officials sometime carry their actions to the extreme. (Who will ever forget the media attention given to the first grade boy who was expelled for kissing a first grade girl on the cheek?) However, teachers should not trivialize sexual harassment complaints or inappropriate sexual conduct (Stein, 1995). As teachers teach students about appropriate classroom behavior, they must also extend their lessons to appropriate social behavior (Hutchison, 2000). Behavior that once would be attributed to "boys will be boys" is no longer tolerated by an enlightened society (Note, 2000, p. 287).

Extended Thinking Activities

Penelope, a 16 year-old sophomore, is quite attractive and receives considerable attention from many of the boys at the school. However, one particular boy, Adrian, has her concerned. Penelope told Ms. Rodriguez, her science teacher, that Adrian has made several suggestive comments to her, and "puts his hands all over her." Penelope also told Ms. Rodriguez that she told him to leave her alone on at least four occasions.

1. Should Adrian's actions be considered sexual harassment? What kinds of questions might Ms. Rodriguez ask Penelope to determine if it is sexual harassment?

2. What should Ms. Rodriguez do, if anything, to prevent any "deliberate indifference" sexual harassment claims?

Chapter 4

Special Education

Introduction

Special education is one of the most litigated areas in public education today (Osborne, 1999; Heubert, 1997). Additionally, it "is a complex and changing area of law" (Borreca, 1996, p. 307). The intrusion of the legal system into special education can be argued as positive or negative, but Cartwright, Cartwright, and Ward (1995) note that "we now have free public education for children with disabilities because it is the law of the land" (p. 12). Tucker (1998) admonishes that special education law was enacted "to address the failure of state education systems to meet the educational needs of children with disabilities" (p. 330).

The primary legislation governing special education is a federal statute, the Individuals with Disabilities Education Act (IDEA). However, Texas law and State Board of Education rules provide guidance to Texas educators regarding all aspects of special education. (See Figure 4.1) These laws and rules are compatible and complementary. A description of these laws and rules can be found in the Texas Education Agency (TEA) publication appropriately entitled the *TEA Side-by-Side*.[1]

Additional guidance for special education is provided by the Office of Special Education and Rehabilitative Services in the U.S. Department of Education through the development of federal regulations and memoranda (Levin, 2000).

The purpose of this chapter is to briefly address special education issues imminently important to the classroom teacher. This chapter will not provide the classroom teacher with the information necessary to obtain a thorough understanding of special education.

---

[1] The *TEA Side-by-Side* can be obtained in PDF format at http://www.tea.state.tx.us/special.ed/rules/idea.html

Figure 4.1
Special Education Laws and Rules

Federal Law

Individuals with Disabilities Education Act (IDEA)
Section 504 of the Rehabilitation Act of 1973

State Law

Texas Education Code, Sections 29.001 – 29.015

State Education Rules

Texas Administrative Code, Title 19 Chapter 89

Students with Disabilities

Teachers often wonder "who is served by special education"? Not all children fall under the IDEA guidelines identifying eligible students (Tucker, 1998). Students with disabilities are those

> With mental retardation, hearing impairments (including deafness), speech or language impairments, visual impairments (including blindness), serious emotional disturbance (hereinafter referred to as "emotional disturbance"), orthopedic impairments, autism, traumatic brain injury, other health impairments, or specific learning disabilities. (20 USCA § 1401 [3][A])

A student does not utilize special education services simply because he or she may fit into one of the above categories. The student must also require special education (or a related service) because of the disability (Rothstein, 2000). Yell (1998) warns "at a minimum, however, all students with disabilities who meet the appropriate criteria as defined in the IDEA categories must receive services" (p. 74).

Classroom teachers will work with students who are classified as learning disabled more than students with other disabilities. Unfortunately, students who are learning disabled are not easily identified, and there is a tendency toward "overidentification" of students in the learning disability category (Rothstein, 2000, p. 80). The prudent teacher will work diligently with the struggling student, other teachers, and the school administration to appropriately assist the student before referring him or her for special education diagnostic testing.[2] Schroth and Littleton (2001) note that referrals are not intended to be the first intervention to assist the student, but teachers should be warned against using the pre-referral interventions as a means to delay the referral (Bateman, 1995).

After exhausting all possible non-special education means to assist the student, continued lack of success on the part of the student might prompt the teacher to refer the student for special education services. This should be done only after consultation with the principal. Texas has specific guidelines regarding the process for referring a student for special education services, and the principal will guide the teacher through the referral process.

The Process

IDEA's purpose is "to ensure that all children with disabilities have available to them a free appropriate public education that emphasizes special education and related services designed to meet their unique needs and prepare them for employment and independent living" (20 USCA § 1400 [d][1][A]). As a result, IDEA established broad parameters for the referral, testing, admission, and dismissal process. Using these parameters, Texas established specific guidelines that each district must follow.

---

[2] Rothstein (2000) aptly notes that categorizing a student in special education can "stigmatize" the child, "and once a child is labeled, it is unlikely that the label for that child will ever be changed" (p. 48).

Step 1: Referral

Parents, medical personnel, or educators can make a student referral for special education services. Generally, classroom teachers refer the students for special education services (Schroth and Littleton, 2001). As discussed previously, this referral is seldom made prior to attempting other interventions in the classroom. A referral document can be obtained from the building principal.

Step 2: Diagnostic Testing

Once a student is referred for diagnostic testing, the school must obtain permission from the parent to test the student. Without parental permission, the process ceases unless the school district chooses to pursue legal avenues to obtain permission for testing (Rothstein, 2000). The results of the assessment will later be used to determine the appropriate services for the student.

Step 3: ARD Committee Meeting

The admission, review, and dismissal (ARD) committee[3] is a group of individuals who determine the appropriate educational plan for special education students. The ARD committee is composed of

- A classroom teacher–usually the one who makes the referral (if such was the case)
- A representative from special education–usually the special education teacher who may be working with the student if the student is admitted to the special education program
- A district representative who can commit resources necessary to assist the student–usually an administrator
- Someone who can interpret assessment data–usually this is an educational diagnostician, and
- Parent or guardian of the student

---

[3] IDEA uses the term Individual Education Program (IEP) team. ARD committee is a term used by Texas educators to refer to the IEP team.

The ARD committee reviews all available data to determine the student's individual education program (IEP) in his or her least restrictive environment (LRE). Once the ARD committee determines the appropriate program, with appropriate classroom modifications, the program is documented on an IEP document. The IEP document is a legal document, and must be strictly followed. The ARD committee must approve deviations from the program as written on the document.

Step 4: Implementation

Once the ARD committee has decided on the appropriate IEP for the child, the school is responsible for implementing the appropriate services and modifications. Classroom teachers must be cognizant of the modifications and services for each student in the special education program.

Upon occasion a school district is required to provide related services to special education students. The United States Code of Federal Regulations defines related services as

> Transportation and such developmental, corrective, and other supportive services as are required to assist a child with a disability to benefit from special education, and includes speech-language pathology and audiology services, psychological services, physical and occupational therapy, recreation, including therapeutic recreation, early identification and assessment of disabilities in children, counseling services, including rehabilitation counseling, orientation and mobility services, and medical services for diagnostic or evaluation purposes. The term also includes school health services, social work services in schools, and parent counseling and training. (CFR § 300.24)

Basically, a related service is any service that a child needs to benefit from special education (Rothstein, 2000). Medical services need not be provided by the school district. Medical services is an ambiguous term that is still being defined by the courts (Fischer, Schimmel, and Kelly, 1999). However, it appears that medical services are those that must be performed by a physician (*Irving v. Tatro*, 1984).

What do I do if a student moves from another district with an IEP established by an ARD committee in that district?

Follow the plan established by the ARD committee in the previous district. Your principal will likely convene an ARD committee to consider the appropriate placement in your school.

Step 5: Review

A student's IEP can be reviewed at any point. At a minimum, the ARD committee must review each student's IEP annually, and the student will undergo a re-evaluation approximately every three years (Borecca, 1999). Typically, an IEP will be reviewed if student progress suggests that the IEP needs to be changed. The student may be progressing exceptionally well, making little or no progress, or engaging in serious or persistent misbehavior.

Classroom Instruction

The classroom teacher is responsible for ensuring that the student's individual education plan is followed. As a result, the teacher must implement any instructional or testing modification outlined in the IEP document.[4] Borecca (1999) cautions that

> Specific day-to-day adjustments in instructional methods and approaches...would not normally require action by the child's IEP team [ARD committee]. However, if changes are contemplated in the child's measurable annual goals, benchmarks, [or] short-term objectives...the school district must ensure that the child's IEP team [ARD committee] is reconvened in a timely manner to address those changes. (p. 31)

---

[4] As discussed later in the chapter, the IEP may include more than directions for instruction. Often the IEP includes directions for behavior modification.

Special education students are to be mainstreamed into the classroom to the extent possible. In other words, special education students should be "in an instructional arrangement with their nondisabled peers as much as possible" (Kemerer and Walsh, 2000, p. 98). The courts have been reluctant to rule against teachers in cases where educational malpractice has been charged. However, in recent years, the courts have shown a willingness to consider these cases in the special education area (Rothstein, 2000). Consequently, sensible teachers take special care to implement modifications and services appropriately.

Currently, special education students can be exempted from state testing requirements (Texas Assessment of Academic Skills) if the ARD committee exempts the student. However, it is the intent of state policymakers that special education students be included, to the extent possible, in the accountability system. The state has developed alternative assessments for special education students, and school districts must explain exemptions to the Texas Education Agency (Murdock, 2000).

Teachers who sponsor or chaperone off-site school activities with special education students should be cautious. A teacher who chaperones such an activity may be unaware of modifications or related services required by the school. For example, a student may require clean intermittent catheterization (CIC) provided by the school as a related service. Failure to perform the CIC may not only prove harmful to the health of the student, but may open the district to liability (*Irving v. Tatro*, 1984).

Student Discipline

The discipline of special education students is probably the most controversial component of all special education legislation. Generally, disabled students are disciplined no differently from non-disabled students (Fischer and Sorenson, 1996); however, no student may be disciplined for behavior that results from his or her disability (Essex, 1999). Underwood and Mead (1995) remind that "one must first determine if there is a nexus between the behavior in question and the disability" (p. 197).

A review of the student's IEP will indicate if the student is to receive special consideration in disciplinary matters. A behavior intervention plan (BIP) may be present as part of the IEP. A BIP is a written set of specific guidelines which provide positive intervention and possibly highly restrictive procedures for the teacher to implement (Bradford, 2001; Rawson, 2000). It is important to note that all teachers, even those who do not interact with the disabled student on a regular basis, are required to follow the behavioral guidelines established in the IEP.

Also, major infractions that lead to placement in an alternative setting may be considered a change in placement, and the ARD committee must approve any change in placement.

Section 504

Section 504 is the term used for a particular section of the Rehabilitation Act of 1973 (29 USCA § 794). Originally considered an employment law, Section 504 bars discrimination against individuals with a disability (Rothestein, 2000). Osborne (1996) points out that a student "is considered to have a disability under section 504 if he or she has a physical or mental impairment that substantially limits one or more major life activities, has a record of such an impairment, or is regarded as having such an impairment" (p. 172). Section 504 not only protects students with a disability, but students who "are 'regarded' as having an impairment" (Underwood and Mead, 1995, p. 42). Schroth and Littleton (2001) note that students with disabilities who are not covered by special education eligibility guidelines continue to be protected by Section 504 provisions.

Students who qualify for Section 504 services may have dyslexia, short-term illnesses, asthma, heart disease, or other similar disabilities that may not lead to special education services (Tucker, 1998). Teachers must provide reasonable accommodations for these students. Although Section 504 does not afford the student the same amount of protection that IDEA does, teachers have the same legal obligation to provide modifications for students receiving Section 504 services.

What is a reasonable accommodation?

There is no definition of what is reasonable. Yell (1999) tells us that "determining what constitutes a reasonable accommodation ... is difficult and subjective. What is reasonable will vary given the specifics of a particular situation" (p. 106). Use good judgment. How could a teacher accommodate for a student whose writing hand is placed in a cast? The teacher might allow the student to use a tape recorder or have another student assist with class notes. As can be seen, reasonableness is limited only by the creativity of the teacher, student, and parents.

Each school district must have a Section 504 coordinator (Yell, 1999). Teachers who need additional assistance with reasonable accommodations and appropriate modifications should contact the district coordinator.

Summary

Laws, rules, and administrative guidelines regarding students in special populations can be quite confusing. Additionally, it is discomforting to learn that litigation in these areas is increasing at a rapid pace. It is incumbent upon the teacher to be aware of the laws and regulations governing special programs, and to follow the guidelines carefully.

Extended Thinking Activities

Amanda Jackson is a 9th grade student with an emotional disturbance disability. She and Rowanda Adams, a regular education student, were found in the girls' restroom smoking cigarettes. Rowanda admitted guilt. Amanda admitted smoking a cigarette, but indicated that her psychiatrist told her to "light one up" when she was nervous. "It will help you keep calm," she said the psychiatrist told her. The student code of conduct requires a five-day stay in the Alternative Education Center for having tobacco on campus.

1. What must be considered prior to implementing the discipline for Amanda and Rowanda?

2. Would removal to the Alternative Education Center result in a change of placement for Amanda?

Chapter 4

Demonstrate Your Knowledge

Circle T if the statement is true and F if the statement is false.

T   F   1. If IDEA guidelines and state special education regulations conflict, the teacher must follow the state regulations.

T   F   2. Special education is the most litigated aspect of public education.

T   F   3. Teachers should attempt intervention strategies prior to referring a student for special education services.

T   F   4. Before a student can be evaluated (tested) for special education services, the parent must agree.

T   F   5. The ARD committee only approves major changes in the student's IEP.

T   F   6. A student's IEP must be reviewed at least every 3 years.

T   F   7. A teacher is legally bound to implement the modifications listed in a student's IEP.

T   F   8. Regardless of the disability, special education students must be disciplined in the same manner as a non-special education student for the same infraction.

T   F   9. Section 504 is an employment law that relates to accommodations for employees and not for students.

T   F   10. Under Section 504, a person need only to be perceived to have a disability to be protected from discrimination.

Chapter 5

Educational Records

Introduction

Teachers interact daily with various types of educational records. Indeed, teachers create abundant educational records by the very act of performing their instructional responsibilities. However, teachers often are unaware of the information that must be confidential and the information that must be made available to others (Clark, 2001). This chapter will provide teachers with a basic understanding of educational records, the laws that govern their release, and the teacher's role in maintaining the records.

Laws Governing Educational Records

In Texas, there are two laws that directly affect access to student records (Scott, 2000). The Texas Public Information Act (Texas Government Code § 552) is the state statute that provides guidance to educators regarding access to educational records. The Family Rights and Privacy Act (FERPA) is the federal statute controlling access to educational records (20 U.S.C.A. 1232g). Although they are separate statutes, the statutes overlap greatly and it is difficult to discuss educational records without referring to both.

Texas Public Information Act

Scott (2000) tells us that the purpose of the Texas Public Information Act (TPIA) "is to give the public full and complete information regarding the affairs of government and the official acts of those who represent them as public officials and employees" (p. 12). The TPIA incorporates all of the provisions of the federal statute, FERPA, (Kemerer and Walsh, 2000) and "does not require the release of information contained in education

records of an education agency or institution, except in conformity with [FERPA]" (Texas Government Code [TGC] § 552.026).
Basically, the TPIA

1. Provides the public with the authority to access all educational records generated by a school, and
2. Prohibits access to educational records of an individual student by anyone except the parent, educational personnel, and individuals conducting a child abuse investigation.

Does this mean that all of my notes, even my personal notes, are open to the public?

In 1975, the Texas Attorney General decided that personal notes of an individual would not be considered public records subject to release (Open Records Decision Number 77). Unfortunately, there is no "bright line" separation between personal notes and educational records. For example, a teacher who makes notes about student behavior in the class, yet keeps those notes in a personal binder is probably creating an educational record and not personal notes. Scott (2000) warns us that "the general rule of thumb is that, if the documents are important enough to maintain, they are official documents and may have to be released" (p. 14).

The following are generally not considered educational records:

- Records of instructional, or supervisory personnel which are the sole possession of the maker
- Law enforcement records if the enforcement agency is part of the educational institution,[1] and

---

[1] Scott (2000) warns that law enforcement records placed in a student's folder becomes subject to FERPA.

- Records of a person who is an employee of, but not in attendance at the educational institution. (20 U.S.C.A. 1232g [a] [4] [B])

Family Educational Rights and Privacy Act

Congress passed the Family Educational Rights and Privacy Act (FERPA) in 1974 to regulate the release of student records. FERPA is not designed to replace state law (Valente and Valente, 2001), but it provides parents with almost unlimited access to student records while restricting access to others. FERPA defines an educational record as "records, files, documents and other materials which contain information directly related to a student; and are maintained by an educational agency or institution or by a person acting for such agency or institution" (20 U.S.C.A. § 1232g [4] [A]).

Valente and Valente (2001) remind us that FERPA requires schools to 1) provide parents access to all school records concerning their child, 2) allow parents an opportunity to appeal student records that are incorrect, and 3) let the parents include a written response to any educational record that they deem incorrect.

Access to Educational Records

Parents and eligible students[2] have access to the student's educational records. Educational records are more than documents written on paper. Teachers in possession of educational records must "permit access to or the release, transfer, or other communication of personally identifiable information contained in education records to any party, by any means, including oral, written, or electronic means" (43 CFR § 99.3).

Some educational records can be made available to the population in general provided that the information is not personally identifiable. For example, a teacher may post grades on an exam or for a grading period, but the grades must not be

---

[2] An eligible student is one who "has reached 18 years of age or is attending an institution of postsecondary education" (34 CFR § 99.3).

matched to the students in a manner that identifies the students (Mawdsley, 2000). Therefore, using information such as a social security number or student identification number in which students can identify other students is a violation of FERPA (34 CFR § 99.3).

Should I not use the students' social security numbers when I post grades?

No, you should not. However, you may give the student a personal identification number known only to the two of you and post the grades accordingly.

There are exceptions to FERPA in which individuals or institutions may have access to a student's educational records. According to Scott (2000), those include:

- School officials who have a legitimate educational interest
- School officials from other schools in which the student intends to enroll
- Accrediting organizations, and
- Persons or grand juries who have subpoenaed the records

It is possible that others can access a student's educational records. Parents (or eligible student) may provide access to the student's educational records to a third party with written permission specifying which records may be accessed (34 CFR § 99.30).

Confidentiality of Records

If the education records of a student contain information on other students, then the parent (or eligible students) can have access to only the information about that student. It would be a of FERPA to allow access to the information about the other students without written permission.

Information that is considered directory information is not subject to the confidentiality requirements of FERPA. The Code of Federal Regulations defines directory information as

> Information contained in an education record of a student which would not generally be considered harmful or an invasion of privacy. It includes ... name, address, telephone listing, date and place of birth, [and] major field of study ... (34 CFR § 99.3)

Parents must be given an annual opportunity to restrict directory information (34 CFR § 99.7). Furthermore, non-custodial parents must be provided access to their children's educational records unless a "legally binding document ... specifically revokes these rights" (34 CFR § 99.4). A parent does not have the authority to instruct "school personnel to deny access to the child's other parent" (Scott, 2000, p. 5).

I notice that programs distributed at football and basketball games lists the names of the athletes, their height and weight. Isn't that an unauthorized release of personally identifiable information?

No. Listing names of those participating in officially recognized sports and activities, along with the height and weight of the athletes, is considered directory information.

Electronic mail, or email, can lead to interesting FERPA discussions. Information exchanged between two teachers about a student's grade is not a violation of FERPA if both teachers have a legitimate educational interest. However, if the email is forwarded to others on the email server, then the disclosure provisions of FERPA are violated.

The long-standing teacher practice of allowing students to grade each other's papers has come under scrutiny by the courts. In

Falvo v. Owasso Independent School District (2000), the 10th Circuit Court ruled that the practice of allowing students to grade each others' papers violated FERPA.[3]

Summary

Most documents created and kept on file by teachers are considered educational records. These records are open to inspection by some, yet prohibited from inspection by others. Generally, teachers should allow parents to inspect the records kept on their children, but not allow the inspection of another child's records.

Extended Thinking Activities

After several grading periods indicating excellent performance, Rosalinda's academic performance slips. Her math grades continue to be quite good, but her science and social studies grades dropped considerably. You spoke with her mother via the telephone and indicated that her test grades proved to be the culprit. Rosalinda is diligent in completing her homework. Now, her mother has arrived at the school and insists that she be allowed to see your grade book. She wants to discover how well the other students in the class did in comparison with Rosalinda.

1. Do you allow Rosalinda's mother to view your grade book? Why or why not?
2. Is there any way that you can report Rosalinda's progress in comparison with her classmates?

---

[3] The Family Compliance Office has determined that a videotape made by school officials is an educational record.

Chapter 5

Demonstrate Your Knowledge

Circle T if the statement is true and F if the statement is false.

T F 1. The Texas statute governing educational records is called the Family Educational Rights and Privacy Act.

T F 2. The Texas Public Information Act provides parents with access to their child's educational records.

T F 3. Allowing students to grade each other's papers has been held a violation of FERPA.

T F 4. School officials must obtain a written release before they can obtain educational records from a previous school.

T F 5. If the parents are divorced, the non-custodial parent does not have access to the child's records unless access is granted by the custodial parent.

T F 6. Parents (or eligible students) have the right to restrict directory information.

T F 7. A student's name, address, and date of birth is generally considered directory information.

T F 8. Parents (or eligible students) can issue access to educational records with written permission.

T F 9. Education records (e.g., posting of exam grades) that are not personally identifiable can be made available to the general population.

T F 10. Personal notes, taken by a supervisor and maintained in the sole possession of the supervisor, are not considered educational records.

Chapter 6

Educator Code of Ethics

Introduction

Rule Number 2 states that *Just because something is legal, it doesn't mean that it is "right."* The educator code of ethics is designed to address this rule. Teachers are constantly faced with ethical dilemmas. Teachers seldom have difficulty with choices of right vs. wrong. However, choices of right vs. right often provide greater consternation[1] (McNaughten, McCreight, Gonzalez, and Beach, 2000).

The Texas State Board for Educator Certification (SBEC) adopted the Educator Code of Ethics and is the state agency responsible for its enforcement.

Code of Ethics for Educators in Texas

Although some professionals view ethics codes as "rules designed to hinder practice," the "codes become moral standards … and provide practitioners with a guide to making ethical decisions" (Parson, 2001, p. 41). Title 19 Chapter 247 of the Texas Administrative Code (TAC) consists of the Code of Ethics and Standard Practices for Texas Educators.

Principle I – Professional Ethical Conduct

The Texas educator shall maintain the dignity of the profession by respecting and obeying the law, demonstrating personal integrity, and exemplifying honesty.

Standard 1. The educator shall not intentionally misrepresent official policies of the school district or educational

---

[1] "Right" as discussed here is not a legal or constitutional right, but what is correct or good for an individual or society.

institution and shall clearly distinguish those views from personal attitudes and opinions.

Standard 2. The educator shall honestly account for all funds committed to his or her charge and shall conduct financial business with integrity.

Standard 3. The educator shall not use institutional or professional privileges for personal or partisan advantage.

Standard 4. The educator shall accept no gratuities, gifts, or favors that impair professional judgment.

Standard 5. The educator shall not offer any favor, service, or thing of value to obtain special advantage.

Standard 6. The educator shall not falsify records, or direct or coerce others to do so.

Principle II – Professional Practices and Performance

The Texas educator, after qualifying in a manner established by law or regulation, shall assume responsibilities for professional administrative or teaching practices and professional performance and shall demonstrate competence.

Standard 1. The educator shall apply for, accept, offer, or assign a position or a responsibility on the basis of professional qualifications and shall adhere to the terms of a contract or appointment.

Standard 2. The educator shall not deliberately or recklessly impair his or her mental or physical health or ignore social prudence, thereby affecting his or her ability to perform the duties of his or her professional assignment.

Standard 3. The educator shall organize instruction that seeks to accomplish objectives related to learning.

Standard 4. The educator shall continue professional growth.

Standard 5. The educator shall comply with written local school board policies, state regulations, and other applicable state and federal laws.

Principle III – Ethical Conduct Toward Professional Colleagues

The Texas educator, in exemplifying ethical relations with colleagues, shall accord just and equitable treatment to all members of the profession.

Standard 1. The educator shall not reveal confidential information concerning colleagues unless disclosure serves lawful professional purposes or is required by law.

Standard 2. The educator shall not willfully make false statements about a colleague or the school system.

Standard 3. The educator shall adhere to written local school board policies and state and federal laws regarding dismissal, evaluation, and employment processes.

Standard 4. The educator shall not interfere with a colleague's exercise of political and citizenship rights and responsibilities.

Standard 5. The educator shall not discriminate against, coerce, or harass a colleague on the basis of race, color, religion, national origin, age, sex, disability, or family status.

Standard 6. The educator shall not intentionally deny or impede a colleague in the exercise or enjoyment of any professional right or privilege.

Standard 7. The educator shall not use coercive means or promise of special treatment in order to influence professional decisions or colleagues.

Standard 8. The educator shall have the academic freedom to teach as a professional privilege, and no educator shall interfere with such privilege except as required by state and/or federal laws.

Principle IV – Ethical Conduct Toward Students

The Texas educator, in accepting a position of public trust, should measure success by progress of each student toward realization of his or her potential as an effective citizen.

Standard 1. The educator shall deal considerately and justly with each student and shall seek to resolve problems including discipline according to law and school board policy.

Standard 2. The educator shall not intentionally expose the student to disparagement.

Standard 3. The educator shall not reveal confidential information concerning students unless disclosure serves lawful professional purposes or is required by law.

Standard 4. The educator shall make reasonable effort to protect the student from conditions detrimental to learning, physical health, mental health, or safety.

Standard 5. The educator shall not deliberately distort facts.

Standard 6. The educator shall not unfairly exclude a student from participation in a program, deny benefits to a student, or grant an advantage to a student on the basis of race, color, sex, disability, national origin, religion, or family status.

Standard 7. The educator shall not unreasonably restrain the student from independent action in the pursuit of learning or deny the student access to varying points of view.

Principle V – Ethical Conduct Toward Parents and Community

The Texas educator, in fulfilling citizenship responsibilities in the community, should cooperate with parents and others to improve the public schools of the community.

Standard 1. The educator shall make reasonable effort to communicate to parents information that lawfully should be revealed in the interest of the student. (With the exception of child abuse reporting, parents are legally entitled to all information concerning the school activities of their child and teachers cannot coerce a child to withhold information from the parents [Texas Education Code § 26.008]).

Standard 2. The educator shall endeavor to understand community cultures and relate the home environment of students to the school.

Standard 3. The educator shall manifest a positive role in school-public relations.

Reporting Ethics Violations

Each year the State Board for Educator Certification (SBEC) places on the investigative docket approximately 2,000 incidents involving Texas educators. Although that number represents less than 1% of the practicing educators in Texas, the number is still quite large. Because of the large number of investigations on the docket and the small number of investigators assigned to the investigative tasks, SBEC prioritizes the investigations and any subsequent certificate actions. Naturally, the most heinous incidents get the top priority.

Teaching is about working with people. Occasionally, personality conflicts will arise or interpersonal conflicts will create tension between individuals. Parsons (2001) notes that "by themselves, ethical standards do not always provide clear choices for helpers to avoid conflict, make the best decisions for all involved and maintain freedom from legal entanglement (p. 41).[2]

Prior to filing a code of ethics complaint, the teacher should identify the specific standard violated. Failure to do so is, in essence, filing an unsubstantiated complaint, and may well be a violation of the code of ethics (Principal III, Standard 2). Teachers should make every possible attempt to resolve violations locally. Teachers should utilize personal communication skills, conflict resolution strategies, or other tactful means to address code violations. It may be necessary to report violations to a supervisor who can use informal leadership skills or a formal leadership position. However, some violations of the code of ethics are so persistent, pervasive, or severe that filing a complaint with SBEC is the only avenue for resolution.

Filing a Code of Ethics Complaint

Teachers must avoid filing a code of ethics complaint because of a personality conflict, professional jealousy, or philosophical differences in instructional methodology. Also, teachers must avoid filing a complaint against a supervisor based

---

[2] Instructions for filing a code of ethics complaint can be found at the State Board for Educator Certification website: http://www.sbec.state.tx.us.

upon an adverse administrative decision when the decision is within the supervisor's authority. Such filings seldom lead to a better working environment and often lead to an acrimonious relationship. *The keys to filing complaints are 1) evidence of a violation, and 2) a clear relationship between the action and a standard in the code of ethics.*

Figure 6.1
When Not to File a Code of Ethics Complaint

- Avoid filing a complaint against a colleague because of professional jealousy.
- Avoid filing a complaint against a colleague because of a personality conflict.
- Avoid filing a compliant against a colleague because of a philosophical difference in instructional methodology.
- Avoid filing a complaint against a supervisor because of an adverse administrative decision within the supervisor's authority.

Steps in the Complaint Process

Wagner (1996) notes that "a code of ethics will not supply specific answers to specific problems, but it will provide the principles and directions to be taken in solving an ethical problem" (p. 32). Good people disagree about what is ethical and what is not. As a result, SBEC has established a process for resolving conflicting points of view in a professional manner (see Figure 6.2). The complaint process is established in Texas Administrative Code (19 TAC § 249). It must be noted that the person filing the complaint can withdraw the complaint at any time.

Step 1. When two educators have a disagreement over an action that is rooted in the code of ethics, the educators should try to resolve the issue before involving SBEC personnel.

Step 2. If all reasonable attempts to resolve the conflict at the local level fail, the teacher may then file a report with SBEC.

At the SBEC website, teachers can obtain a copy of a complaint form that is to be completed and submitted to the state.[3] Once submitted, SBEC considers the complaint as an "alleged violation."

So, if I observe another educator slapping a student across the face, I should try to resolve the issue locally and not involve SBEC?

No, SBEC should be involved. Severe violations of the Code of Ethics should be reported.

Step 3. Once the complaint is filed, the person making the complaint must certify to SBEC that he or she has notified the accused educator that a complaint has been filed against him or her. The complainant must also inform the superintendent[4] of the accused that a complaint has been filed. SBEC then provides a 45-day period for the superintendent to address the complaint. The superintendent may institute local resolution processes or may do nothing. However, *only the person filing the complaint can withdraw the complaint.*

Step 4. If the complaint is not withdrawn after the 45-day local resolution period, then the executive director of SBEC will review the complaint. If the executive director determines that the complaint is within the jurisdiction of the commissioner of education, the local board, a court, or if the complaint fails to address a violation of the code of ethics, then the executive director will dismiss the complaint[5]. Otherwise, the executive director will direct the staff to investigate the complaint and within

---

[3] The mailing address for SBEC is State Board for Educator Certification, 1001 Trinity, Austin, Texas 78701.

[4] If the superintendent is the person accused of violating the code of ethics, then the copy of the complaint is sent to the president of the board of trustees.

[5] The executive director may also dismiss a complaint that has no basis in fact or law, or filed only to harass another (19 TAC, § 249.53).

90 days file a petition with the State Office of Administrative Hearings (SOAH) on behalf of the person making the complaint.[6]

Step 5. The complainant may appeal the executive director's dismissal to the SBEC Review Committee. The review committee is composed of three members (a teacher member, an administrator or counselor representative, and a citizen member) of the SBEC. The Review Committee will review the appeal.
Obviously, this step is skipped if the executive director does not dismiss the complaint.

Step 6. The Review Committee may 1) dismiss the complaint, or 2) direct the executive director to file a petition with SOAH. The executive director will then instruct the investigative staff to investigate the complaint and file a petition with SOAH within 90 days. The decision of the Review Committee cannot be appealed.

Step 7. After the complaint is sent to SOAH, an administrative judge will establish a hearing date, hear the complaint (and response from the accused), and issue a proposal for decision. The proposal for decision is sent to the full membership of the SBEC.

Step 8. The final decision-maker of the complaint process is the full membership of the SBEC[7]. The SBEC will review only the proposal for the decision, and the record that accompanies the proposal. (In other words, no oral or written arguments are submitted to the full board.)

---

[6] Only SBEC can file a petition with SOAH.
[7] Board members who served on the Review Committee cannot participate in the final decision of the complaint.

Figure 6.2

Stages in the Complaint Process

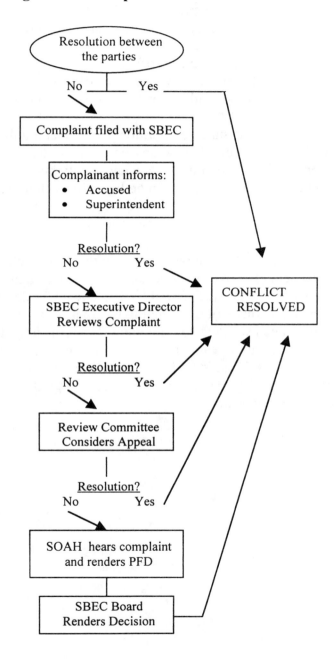

As a result of the complaint, the Texas Administrative Code (19 TAC, § 249.56 [c]) allows the SBEC to

- Place restrictions on the certificate
- Issue a reprimand that may be inscribed on the certificate
- Suspend the certificate
- Revoke or cancel the certificate, or
- Impose additional restrictions upon the certificate.

As was stated earlier, the person making the complaint can withdraw the complaint at any time. Figure 6.2 shows the many steps in the complaint process, and highlights the places in the steps where a complaint can be logically withdrawn.

Summary

Ethical dilemmas abound in the public school classroom. Teachers often face the question of "What is right?" more than they address the question of "What is legal?" Classroom veterans develop a knack of determining the appropriate actions to take when faced with ethical dilemmas. Unfortunately, this "knack" is developed after years of trial-and-error accompanied by "bumps and bruises." The State Board for Educator Certification publishes the Educator Code of Ethics as an ethical guideline for teachers and other educators.

Extended Thinking Activities

Mr. Alexander is a fellow teacher. His students constantly complain about his rigidity in class. Mr. Alexander requires the students to sit in their desks with both feet firmly on the floor underneath the desks. The desks are arranged in rows, and the students must sit in alphabetical order. When writing, students may not have more than one book on the desktop at any time. The students must write in black ink (ink of any other color is strictly prohibited), and errors require that the student rewrite the entire page. He requires the students to raise a hand before speaking, and when called upon, the students must request permission to speak. Everyone in the room is addressed by Mr. or Ms. It is your observation that he is quite harsh with students who speak out of turn.

1. Is Mr. Alexander violating any component of the code of ethics?
2. What would you do, if anything, about Mr. Alexander's rigid manner of classroom management?

Chapter 6

Demonstrate Your Knowledge

Circle T if the statement is true and F if the statement is false.

T   F   1.   The State Board of Education is responsible for enforcing the code of ethics in Texas.

T   F   2.   The code of ethics addresses only what is legal, not what is right.

T   F   3.   A code of ethics always provides specific answers to what are often complicated issues.

T   F   4.   When two educators have a philosophical disagreement regarding instructional methodology, it is best to use the code of ethics complaint process to resolve the instructional issue.

T   F   5.   Filing an unsubstantiated code of ethics complaint is, itself, a violation of the code of ethics.

T   F   6.   There is no appeal of the SBEC executive director's decision to dismiss a code of ethics complaint.

T   F   7.   SOAH provides administrative law judges to render proposals for decision on code of ethics complaints.

T   F   8.   Only SBEC may file a petition with SOAH to hear a code of ethics complaint.

T   F   9.   The Review Committee of the SBEC is the final decision maker on code of ethics complaints.

T   F   10. The superintendent can withdraw a code of ethics complaint made by one of his or her teachers provided a thorough investigation has been conducted at the local level.

Chapter 7

Contracts and Employment

Introduction

Most beginning teachers have a very clear understanding of the amount of their salary. However, most have very little knowledge of contracts offered to Texas teachers. Fewer still realize that a school district is not bound by an employment offer made by an administrator, but only by its approval by the board of trustees.

Contract and employment for public school teachers are controlled by state law and administrative regulations (Alexander and Alexander, 2000). Texas law specifically provides for three types of teacher contracts – probationary, continuing, and term (Texas Education Code [TEC] §§ 21.101 – 21.213). This chapter will discuss the types of contracts and selected employment issues related to Texas teachers.

Types of Contracts

Contract law is a sophisticated area of law. In order to avoid complicated legalese, this chapter will discuss contract law only in its most basic form, and related specifically to contracts relevant to Texas teachers.

Alexander and Alexander (2000) define a contract "as an agreement between two or more competent persons for a legal consideration on a legal subject matter in the form required by law" (p. 668). By law, a teacher who is new to the profession or new to the district must begin on a probationary contract. After a successful period of time on a probationary contract, the teacher is then offered either a continuing contract or a term contract.

Probationary Contracts

A probationary contract may not exceed one year in length. It is intended for teachers who have not been previously employed by the district or who have not been employed by the district for at least two consecutive years (TEC § 21.102).

Beginning Teachers. Teachers new to the profession (and, by definition, new to the district), must be placed on a one-year probationary contract. Upon satisfactory performance, the teacher may be offered additional one-year probationary contracts the following two years (TEC § 21.102 [b]). *Consequently, all beginning teachers will start their Texas teaching careers with a total of three years on a probationary contract.*

At the end of the three years (three one-year contracts), the district may offer the teacher a continuing or term contract. In some instances, a teacher may be on a probationary contract for four years. Kemerer and Walsh (2000) note that "if the board decides to extend probation for a fourth year ... the board of trustees must actually 'determine' and 'recite' that it is in doubt whether the educator should be given a continuing [or term] contract" (p. 128).

What happens if I teach two years with District A and then move to District B? Will District B place me on a probationary contract for three years?

Yes. Unless the teacher has taught in public education for five of the preceding eight years, the teacher must be placed on a probationary contract for three consecutive years.

Experienced Teachers. In some situations, experienced teachers will be offered probationary contracts. Texas law requires "that the probationary period may not exceed one year for a person who has been employed as a teacher in public education for at least five of the previous eight years" (TEC § 21.102 [b]). This means that teachers who are new to a district or who have not been teaching with the district for two consecutive years will be placed on a probationary contract.

Continuing Contracts

A continuing contract is a contract that carries over from one year to the next without board action and without a specified contract period (Kemerer and Walsh, 2000). Continuing contracts effectively provide tenure for public school teachers. Texas Education Code §§ 21.151 – 21.21.160 provide the statutory guidance for continuing contracts.

Term Contracts

Term contracts in the public schools of Texas are very common. Under Texas law, "a term contract' means any contract of employment for a fixed term between a school district and a teacher" (TEC § 21.201 [2]).

The period of time for a term contract may be one or more years, but the term may not exceed five years (TEC § 21.205). Term contracts for Texas teachers are usually one to three years.

All of our teachers are on three-year term contracts. However, each spring the board of trustees "extends" the contracts for another three years. Aren't they really continuing contracts?

No. The contracts are term contracts. The board of trustees, and probably the administration, is showing confidence in the teacher when the contract is "extended." If the practice is common in the district, the failure of the board of trustees to extend a contract may be an ominous sign for the teacher.

Contract Non-Renewal

Since continuing contracts do not have a renewal provision, they are not subject to contract non-renewal. However, teachers who have a term contract are subject to non-renewal.

Under state law, a district must notify the teacher, in writing, at least 45 days prior to the last instructional day whether or not the board plans to renew or non-renew the teacher's contract. Failure to notify the teacher in a timely fashion requires the board to employ the teacher under the same conditions as the previous year (TEC § 21.206).

Boards of trustees who are timely in notifying a teacher of the intent to non-renew must provide the teacher with the opportunity to have a hearing before the board. The board must provide for a hearing within 15 days of the notice unless the teacher and the board agree on an alternate date. Also, the hearing before the board must be a closed meeting unless the teacher requests an open meeting (TEC § 21.207).

If the teacher does not appeal the intent to non-renew within 15 days of receiving the notice, then the board must notify the teacher of their decision (renew or non-renew) within 30 days of the notice. If the teacher requests the hearing, then the board must inform the teacher of its decision within 15 days of the hearing date (TEC § 21.208).

Texas Education Code § 21.209 notes that "a teacher who is aggrieved by a decision of a board of trustees on the nonrenewal of the teacher's term contract may appeal to the commissioner for a review of the decision." The commissioner cannot overturn the decision of the board unless the decision was "arbitrary, capricious, unlawful or not supported by substantial evidence."

Employment Issues

Dismissal

Teachers can be discharged during the contract period for good cause. The Texas Education Code (§§ 21.104, 21.156) defines good cause as "the failure to meet the accepted standards of conduct for the profession." Teachers who are dismissed are provided the opportunity for a hearing before a state hearing examiner as long as the request for the hearing is in a timely manner.

Piskin (1996) notes the following about the hearing process:

- Within 15 days of receiving notice of proposed dismissal, the teacher requests the hearing in writing
- The Commissioner of Education assigns a hearing examiner within 10 business days of the request
- The hearing is held within the geographical boundaries of the district
- The district pays for the costs of the hearing
- The hearing is closed unless the teacher requests it to be open
- The hearing is conducted in the manner of a jury-less trial,
- The district has the burden of proof in the case
- The teacher has the right to legal counsel
- Upon the decision of the hearing examiner, the board has 20 days to meet and consider the recommendation of the hearing examiner
- The board must allow each side to present an oral argument
- Within 10 days of the meeting, the board must make a final decision regarding the dismissal

Within 20 days, the teacher can then appeal the decision of the board to the Commissioner of Education[1]. The Commissioner cannot overturn the decision of the board unless the decision was arbitrary, capricious, unlawful, or not supported by evidence. The Commissioner has 30 days to overturn the decision of the board.

Teaching Responsibilities

State law requires that a contract between a teacher and a school district be for a minimum of 10 months and that the teacher

---

[1] The district then has 20 days to respond.

provide a minimum of 187 days of service (TEC § 21.401). In return, teachers are provided with 45 minutes of planning and preparation time daily (TEC § 21.404), a 30 minute duty-free lunch (TEC § 21.405), and 5 days of personal leave per year with no limit on accumulation (TEC § 22.003).

Contract Abandonment

Teachers may resign from a district (without penalty) by filing a written resignation to the board not later than the 45th day prior to the first day of instruction of the following school year (TEC §§ 21.105 [a], 21.160 [a], 21.210 [a]). Also, with the consent of the board, a teacher may resign at any time.

Teachers who resign from a district without board consent and not within the statutory guidelines may be subject to a severe penalty. Failure to abide by the terms of a contract is a clear violation of the Educator Code of Ethics (see Principle II, Standard 1 in Chapter 7).

Certificate Renewal

In the 1980's every certified teacher in Texas was required to take the TECAT to keep his or her certificate. The test was a basic skills test, and it did little to accomplish its legislative mission–to remove unqualified teachers from the classroom. When the State Board for Educator Certification (SBEC) began to devise rules to implement the legislative requirement of certificate renewal, many educators envisioned the infamous TECAT process. However, the certificate renewal process is actually quite different from the TECAT requirement.

Teachers must accrue at least 150 clock hours of continuing education over a 5 year period[2]. Teachers must maintain their own record of continuing education; however SBEC makes a worksheet available to teachers from their website–www.sbec.state.tx.us.

---

[2] One semester hour of university course work is equivalent to 15 clock hours.

Course work from universities is acceptable for continuing education credit, yet continuing education credit is acceptable only from approved providers. Acceptable activities include:

- Workshops, seminars, conferences, and in-service activities designed to enhance the professional knowledge and skills of teachers
- University course work
- Independent study relevant to professional growth (not to exceed 20% of the required clock hours)
- Development of curriculum materials
- Teaching or presenting a continuing professional education activity, and
- Serving as a mentor teacher (not to exceed 30% of the required clock hours).

Summary

It is common for teachers to be unaware of the type of contract under which they operate. The types of contracts and the regulations guiding their enforcement is established by the state and published in the Texas Education Code. Although the contracts vary somewhat, all of the contracts—probationary, term, or continuing—essentially operate under similar guidelines. Teachers should be very cautious when deciding to leave a contract, however. Teachers who abandon a contract not only open themselves to legal repercussions, but open themselves to the political realities of negative future recommendations.

Extended Thinking Activities

Margaret Threwitt is a third year teacher in the Wachitall ISD. Her husband, who works for the U.S. military, is being transferred to a different location in Texas. She wants very badly to move with him, but there are still seven months left in the school year. Furthermore, the distance between the two cities is too great to commute.

1. Is it possible for Margaret to resign from her position with Wachitall ISD in order to accept a position with another district?
2. What would be the ramifications of Margaret's resignation to the district? What are the possible ramifications for Margaret?
3. If Margaret moves to another district, will she be on a probationary certificate? Why or why not?

References

A Parent's Guide to Child Protective Services (CPS) Investigation. (2001). Texas Department of Protective and Regulatory Services. Retrieved February 19, 2001 from the World Wide Web: http://www.tdprs.state.tx.us

Abington v. Schempp, 374 U.S. 203 (1963).

Adams, A.T. (2000). "The Status of School Discipline and Violence." *Annals of the American Academy of Political & Social Science, 567,* 140–157.

Administration of medication by school district employees or volunteer professionals; immunity from liability. (1995). Texas Education Code, Section 22.052.

Aldridge, J. (1998, August). "School District Computer and Internet Use: Cyber Issues for Employees and Students." *Texas School Administrators' Legal Digest,* 14, pp. 1-8, 27.

Alexander, K. and Alexander, M.D. (2001). *American Public School Law,* Fifth edition. Belmont, CA: West/Thomson Learning.

American Academy of Pediatrics. (2000). "Corporal Punishment in Schools." *Pediatrics, 106,* 343.

Assistance to children with disabilities. United States Code of Federal Regulations, Part 300.

Baker v. Owen, 395 F. Supp. 294 (M.D. N.C., 1975).

Bateman, B.D. (1995). *Better IEP's: How to Develop Legally Correct and Educationally Useful Programs.* Longmont, CO: Sopris West.

Bitkensky, S.H. (1999). "Spare the Rod, Embrace Human Rights: International Law's Mandate Against All Corporal Punishment of Children." *Whittier Law Review, 21,* 147–161.

Black's Dictionary of Law. (1979). Fifth Edition. St. Paul, MN: West Publishing Company.

Borreca, C.P. (1999). "Education of Children with Disabilities." In Borecca, C.P., Gregory, R.L., Horner, J.J. and Muzzy, G.H. (Eds.) *Texas School Law: A Practical Guide, 1999 supplement.* Dayton, OH: Education Law Association. pp. 25-42.

Borreca, C.P. (1996). "Education of Children with Disabilities." In K. Frels, J. Horner, B. Camp, and V.L. Robinson (Eds.) *Texas School Law: A Practical Guide.* Topeka, KS: National Organization of Legal Problems in Education. pp. 307-323.

Bradford, C. (2001). "What's the Big IDEA?" *Principal Leadership, 1*, 73-74.

Brown, L.A. (1996). "Copyright Law." In K. Frels, J. Horner, B. Camp, and V.L. Robinson (Eds.) *Texas School Law: A Practical Guide.* Topeka, KS: National Organization of Legal Problems in Education. pp. 85-99.

Brown, L.A. and Gilbert, C.B. (1996) "Religion in the public schools." In K. Frels, J. Horner, B. Camp, and V.L. Robinson (Eds.) *Texas School Law: A Practical Guide.* Topeka, KS: National Organization of Legal Problems in Education. pp. 57-72.

Cartwright, G.P., Cartwright, C.A., and Ward, M.E. (1995), *Educating Special Learners*, Fourth edition. Boston: Wadsworth Publishing Company.

Charles, C.M. (1992). *Building Classroom Discipline.* Fourth edition. White Plains, NY: Longman.

Child Abuse and Neglect Fact Sheet. (2001). Texas Department of Protective and Regulatory Services. Retrieved on February 19, 2001 from the World Wide Web: http://www.tdprs.state.tx.us

Clark, S.G. (2001). "Confidentiality and Disclosure: A Lesson in Sharing." *Principal Leadership, 1*, 40-43.

Copyrights. Limitations on Exclusive Rights: Fair Use. Chapter 17 U.S.C. § 107.

Discipline: Law and Order. (1995). Texas Education Code, Chapter 37.

Doe v. Taylor, 15 F.3d. 443 (1994).

Education of Individuals With Disabilities. United States Code Annotated, Chapter 20, Section 1400 – 1487.

Edwards, L.P. (1996). "Corporal Punishment and the Legal System." *Santa Clara Law Review, 36*, 983–1023.

Emmer, E.T. Evertson, C.M., Clements, B.S., and Worsham, M.E. (1994). *Classroom Management for Secondary Teachers.* Third edition. Boston: Allyn and Bacon.

Engel v. Vitale, 370 U.S. 421 (1962).

Essex, N.L. (1999). *School Law and the Public Schools.* Boston: Allyn and Bacon.

Falvo v. Owasso Independent School District, 220 F. 3d. 1200 (2000).

Family Educational Rights and Privacy Act. (1974). U.S.C.A. 1232g.

Fischer, L., Schimmel, D. and Kelly, C. (1999). *Teachers and the Law.* Fifth edition. New York: Longman.

Fischer, L. and Sorenson, G.P. (1996). *School Law for Counselors, Psychologists, and Social Workers.* White Plains, NY: Longman.

Foreman, T., and Bernet, W. (2000). "A Misunderstanding Regarding the Duty to Report Suspected Abuse," *Child Maltreatment, 5,* 190-197. (From Academic Search Elite: EBSCO Publishing.) Retrieved February, 19, 2001 from World Wide Web: http://www.ehostvgw12.epnet.com

Fowler, L.S., Henslee, D.G., and Hepworth, R.D. (1998). *How it Works...The Texas School Principal's Complete Legal Reference System.* Austin, TX: Leap Year Publishing Co.

Franklin v. Gwinnett County Public Schools, 503 U.S. 60 (1992).

Gebser v. Lago Vista, 524 U.S. 274 (1998).

Gomez, F.C., and Craycraft, K. (1998). *The Legal Handbook for Texas Teachers.* Bulverde, TX: OMNI Publishers, Inc.

Griffith, C. (1998). "Fair Use and Free Speech on the Web." *Information Today, 15,* 18.

Hairston, J.B. (1998). "Sexual Harassment in the Workplace: New Guidance from the Federal Courts." *Texas School Administrators' Legal Digest, 14,* (9), pp. 1-7, 20.

Harris, A.M., and Grooms, K.B. (2000). "A New Lesson Plan for Educational Institutions: Expanded Rules Governing Liability Under Title IX of the Education Amendments of 1972 for Student and Faculty Sexual Harassment." *American University Journal of Gender, Social Policy & The Law. 8,* 575-621.

Heubert, J.P. (1997). "The More We Get Together: Improving Collaboration Between Educators and Their Lawyers." *Harvard Educational Review,* [On-line], *67.* Available: http://www.edreview.org

Hodgkinson, K., and Baginsky, M. (2000). "Child Protection Training in School-Based Initial Teacher Training: A Survey of School-Centered Initial Teacher Training Courses and Their Trainees." *Educational Studies, 26,* 269-281. (From Academic Search Elite: EBSCO Publishing.) Retrieved February, 19, 2001 from World Wide Web: http://www.ehostvgw12.epnet.com

Hutchison, M.D. (2000). "What You Know About and Don't Deal With Can Cost You: A School District's Potential Liability for Student-on-Student Sexual Harassment: Davis v. Monroe County Board of Education." *Missouri Law Review, 65,* pp. 493-513.

Imber, M., and van Geel, T. (2000). *Education Law.* Second Edition. Mahwah, NJ: Lawrence Erlbaum Associate, Publishers.

Imbrogno, A.R. (2000). "Corporal Punishment in America's Public Schools and the U.N. Convention on the Rights of the Child: A Case for Nonratification." *Journal of Law and Education, 29,* 125–147.

Immunity from Liability for Professional Employees. (1995). Texas Education Code, Section 22.051.

Ingraham v. Wright, 430 U.S. 651 (1977).

Irving Independent School District v. Tatro, 486 U.S. 883 (1984).

Kemerer, F. and Walsh, J. (2000). *The Educator's Guide to Texas School Law.* Fifth Edition. Austin: University of Texas Press.

Kirchner, J.T. (1998). "Childhood Spanking and Increased Antisocial Behavior." *American Family Physicial, 57,* 798.

Davis v. Monroe County Board of Education, 120 F.3d. 1390 (11th Circuit, 1997).

Lemon v. Kurtzman, 403 U.S. 602 (1971).

Levesque, R.J.R. (2001). "Cultural Evidence, Child Maltreatment, and the Law." *Child Maltreatment, 5,* 146-161. (From Academic Select Elite: EBSCO Publishing). Retrieved February, 19, 2001 from World Wide Web http://ehostvgw12.epnet.com

Levin, M.I. (Ed.). (2000). *2000 United States School Laws and Rules*. Eagan, MN: West Group.

Mawdsley, R.D. (2000). *Legal Problems of Religious and Private Schools*. Fourth Edition. Dayton, OH: Education Law Association.

McFadden, A.C. and Marsh, G.E. (1992). "A Study of Race and Gender Bias in the Punishment of School Children." *Education & Treatment of Children, 15,* 140 – 147.

McGlinchey, A., Keenan, M. and Dillenburger, K. (2000). "Outline for the Development of a Screening Procedure for Children Who have been Sexually Abused." *Research on Social Work Practice, 10,* 721–748. (From Academic Search Elite: EBSCO Publishing.) Retrieved February 19, 2001 from the World Wide Web: http://ehostvgw12.epnet

McNaughten, D., McCreight, C.K., Gonzalez, H., and Beach, D. (2000). "Ethics and School Administration: A Daunting Task." In Vornberg, J.A. (Ed.), *Texas Public School Organization and Administration: 2000*. Seventh edition. Dubuque, IA: Kendall/Hunt.

Murdock, J. (2000). "Special Education in Texas." In Funkhouser, C.W. (Ed.) *Education in Texas: Policies, Practices, and Perspectives*. Ninth edition. Columbus, OH: Merrill. pp. 317-324.

Murray, K.T. and Evans, C.S. (2000). "U.S. Supreme Court Revisits School Prayer," *NASSP Bulletin, 84,* (620), pp. 73 – 88.

Nogeura, P.A. (1995). "Preventing and Producing Violence: A Critical Analysis of Responses to School Violence." *Harvard Educational Review, 65,* 189–212.

Nondiscrimination on the basis of sex in education programs and activities receiving or benefiting from federal financial assistance, 34 CFR 106.8(b).

Note: Responding to public school sexual harassment in the face of Davis v. Monroe County Board of Education. (2000). *Brigham Young University Education and Law Journal, 2000,* 287-305.

Osborne, A.G., Jr. (1999). "Students with Disabilities." In Russo, C.J. (Ed.) *The Yearbook of Education Law 1999*. Dayton, OH: Education Law Association. pp. 141-179.

Parsons, R.D. (2001). *The Ethics of Professional Practice*. Boston: Allyn & Bacon.

Petzko, V.N. (2001). "Preventing Legal Headaches." *Principal Leadership, 1*, pp. 34-37.

Piskin, J. (1996). "Employment Contracts." In K. Frels, J. Horner, B. Camp, and V.L. Robinson (Eds.) *Texas School Law: A Practical Guide*. Topeka, KS: National Organization of Legal Problems in Education. pp. 217-229.

Public Information. (1993).Texas Government Code, Chapter 552.

Rawson, M.J. (2000). *A Manual of Special Education Law*. Naples, FL: Morgen Publishing.

Redfield, S.E. (2000). *Thinking Like a Lawyer: An Educator's Guide to Legal Analysis and Research*. Concord, NH: Franklin Pierce Law Center.

Richardson, R.C. and Wilcox, D.J. (1994). "Corporal Punishment in Schools: Initial Progress in the Bible Belt." *Journal of Humanistic Counseling Education and Development, 32,* 173–183.

Robinson, V.L. (1996). "Sexual Harassment of Employees." In K. Frels, J. Horner, B. Camp, and V.L. Robinson (Eds.) *Texas School Law: A Practical Guide*. Topeka, KS: National Organization of Legal Problems in Education. pp. 151-165.

Romeo, F.F. (2000). "The Educator's Role in Reporting the Emotional Abuse of Children." *Journal of Instructional Psychology, 27,* 183-187. (From Academic Search Elite: EBSCO

Publishing.) Retrieved February 19, 2001 from World Wide Web: http://www.ehostvgw12.epnet.com

Rothstein, L.F. (2000). *Special Education Law*. Third edition. New York: Longman.

Santa Fe Independent School District v. Doe, 120 S.Ct. 2266 (2000).

Schroth, G. & Littleton, M. (2001). *The Administration and Supervision of Special Programs in Education*. Dubuque, IA: Kendall/Hunt.

Scott, L.R. (2000, December). *Student Records and Student Privacy: Complying with State and Federal Mandates*. Paper presented at the Cross Timbers Conference on School Law and Policy, Stephenville, TX.

Sesno, A.H. (1998). *97 Savvy Secrets for Protecting Self and School: A Practical Guide for Today's Teachers and Administrators*. Thousand Oaks, CA: Corwin Press. (ERIC Document Reproduction Service No. ED 422 640)

Shalaway, L. (1997). *Learning to Teach*. Jefferson City, MO: Scholastic.

Sheppard, N. (1994). "Child Abuse and Neglect." In Funkhouser, C. *Education in Texas: Policies, Practices, and Perspectives*. Seventh edition. Scottscdale, AZ: Gorsuch Scarisbrick Publishers.

Slate, J.R. and Perez, E. (1991). "Corporal Punishment: Used in a discriminatory manner?" *Clearning House, 91*, 362–365.

Stebler, S., Walsh, J., and Kemerer, F. (2000). *The Student Discipline Handbook*. Denton, TX: Texas School Administrator's Legal Digest.

Stein, N. (1995). "Sexual Harassment in School: The Public Performance of Gendered Violence." *Harvard Educational Review*, [On-line], *65*. Available: http://www.edreview.org/issues/harvard

Thomas, G.J. (1992). "Copyrights: The Law, the Teacher, and the Principal." *Brigham Young University Education and Law Journal, 1-24..*

Tucker, B.P. (1998). *Federal Disability Law in a Nutshell* Second edition. St. Paul, MN: West Group.

Underwood, J.K. and Mead, J.F. (1995). *Legal Aspects of Special Education and Pupil Services*. Boston: Allyn and Bacon.

U.S. Department of Education. (2000). "Sexual Harassment Guidance: Harassment of Students by School Employees, Other Students, or Third Parties. 62 FR 12033, Office of Civil Rights. In Levin, M.I. (Ed.) *2000 United States School Laws and Rules*. Eagan, MN: West Group.

Valente, W.D., and Valente, C.M. (2001). *Law in the Schools*. Fifth edition. Columbus, OH: Merrill/Prentice Hall.

Vital Statistics. (2001, January 29). *U.S. News & World Report, 130*, 6. (From Academic Search Elite: EBSCO Publishing.) Retrieved February 19, 2001 from the World Wide Web: http://ehostvgw10.epnet.com

Vockell, E.L. (1991). "Corporal Punishment: The Pros and Cons." *Clearing House, 64*, 278–283.

Wagner, P.A. (1996). *Understanding Professional Ethics*. Phi Delta Kappa Fastback Number 403. Bloomington, IN: Phi Delta Kappa.

Weiss, C.P. (1996). "Curbing Violence or Teaching It: Criminal Immunity for Teachers Who Inflict Corporal Punishment. *Washington University Law Quarterly, 74*, 1251–1289.

Williams, C.S. (1999). "Note: Schools, Peer Sexual Harassment, Title IX, and Davis v. Monroe County Board of Education. *Baylor Law Review, 51*, pp. 1087-1113.

Wong, H., and Wong, R.T. (1991). *The First Days of School*. Sunnyvale, CA: Harry K. Wong Publications.

Valente, W.D., and Valente, C.M. (2001). *Law in the Schools*, Fifth edition. Columbus, OH: Merrill/Prentice Hall.

Yell, M.L. (1998). *The Law and Special Education*. Columbus, OH: Merrill.